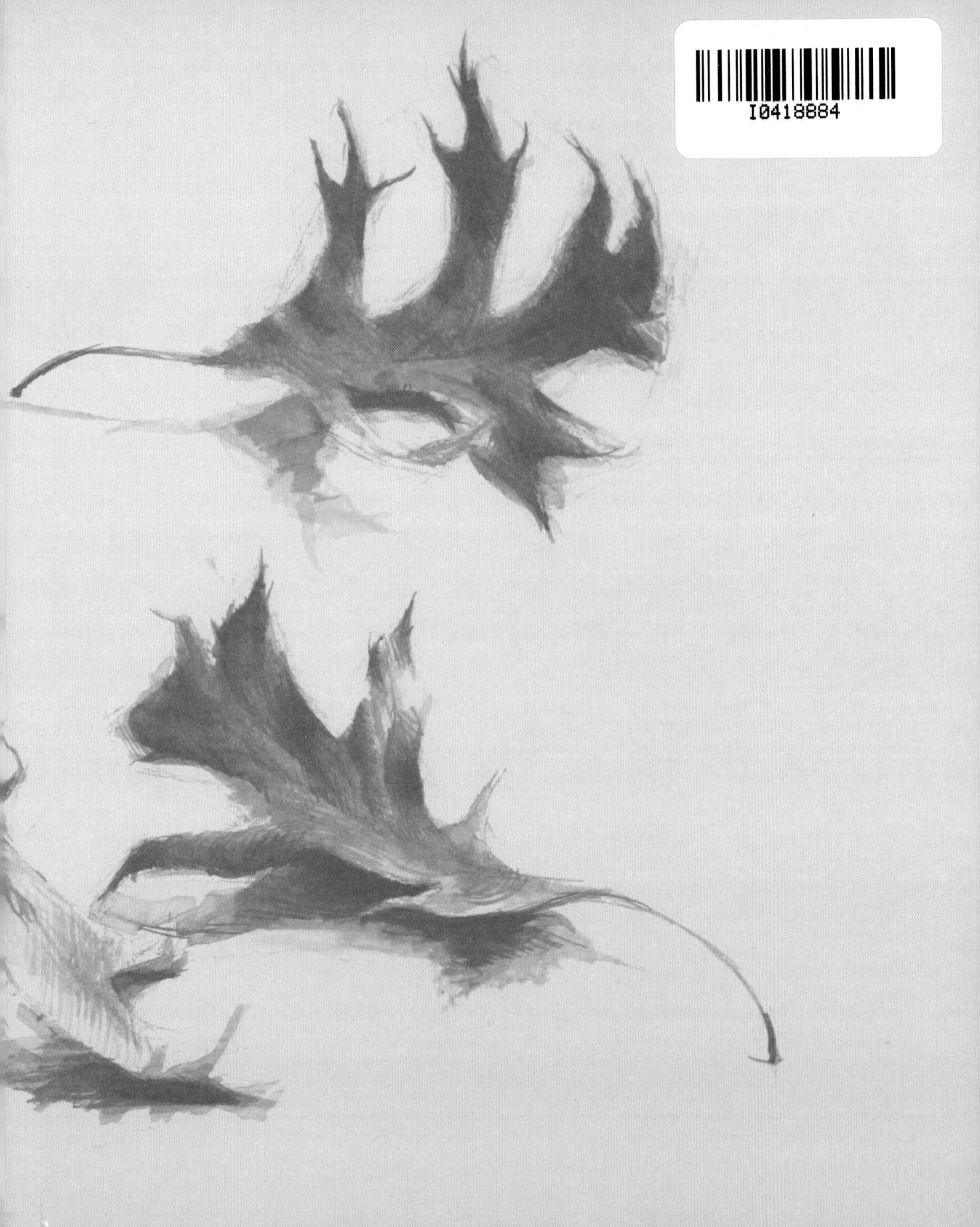

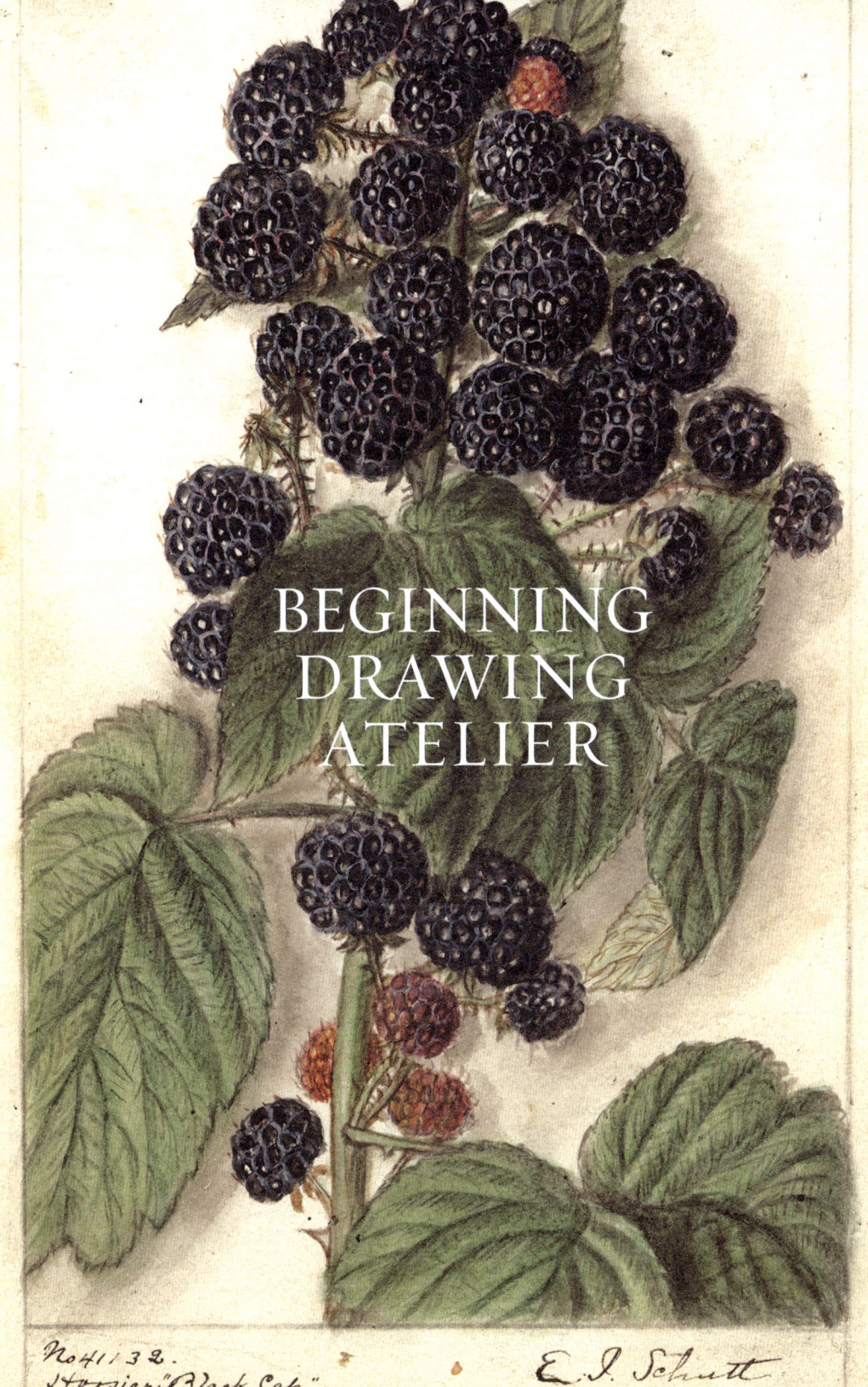

BEGINNING
DRAWING
ATELIER

No 41132.
Horsier "Black Cap"
Alvin & Gray.

E. I. Schutt
July 9 '08

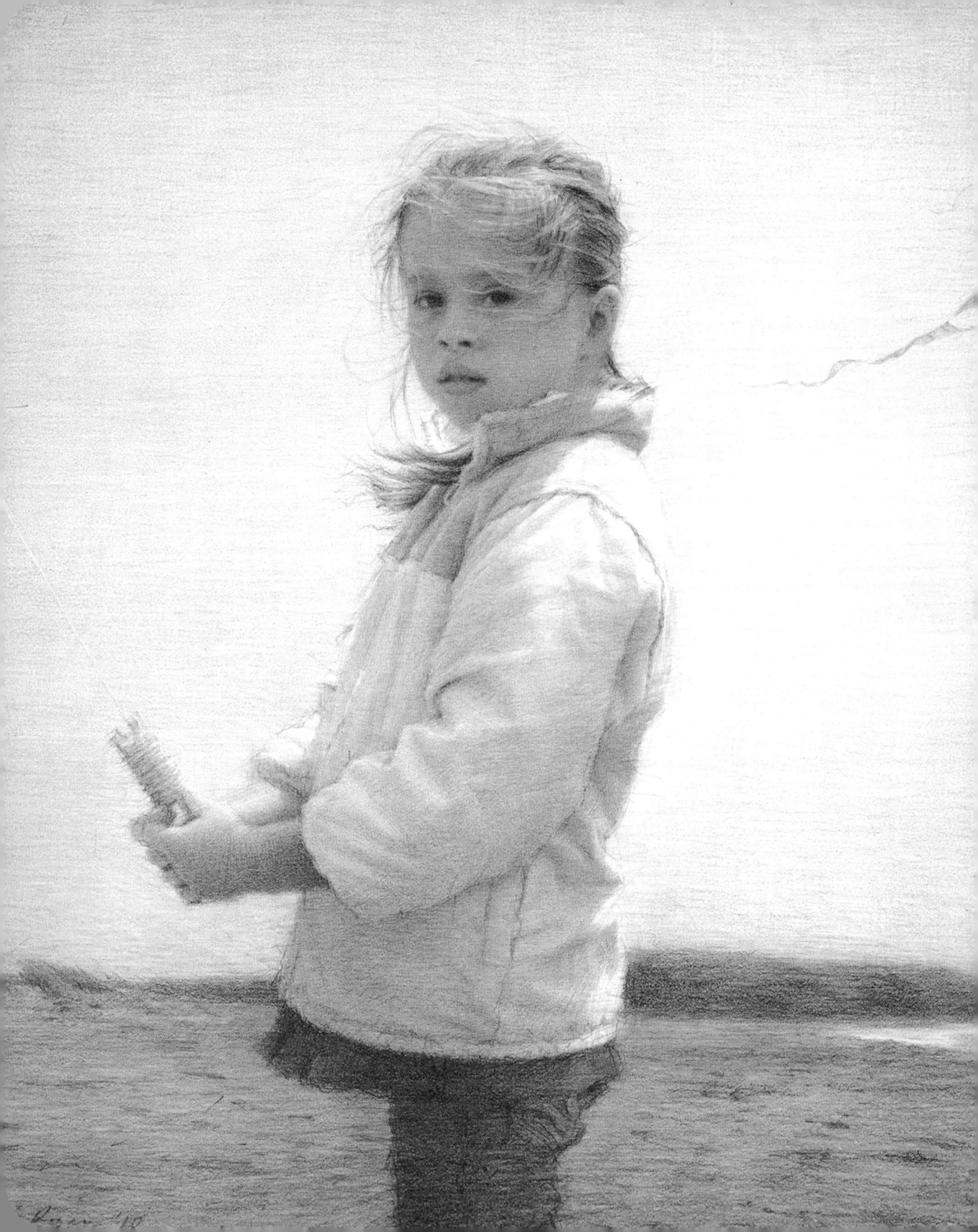

BEGINNING DRAWING ATELIER

An Instructional Sketchbook

Juliette Aristides

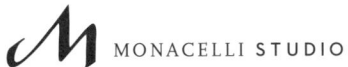

MONACELLI STUDIO

Library of Congress Cataloging-in-Publication Data

Names: Aristides, Juliette, author.
Title: Beginning drawing atelier : an instructional sketchbook /
Juliette Aristides.
Description: First edition. | New York : Monacelli Studio, 2019.
Identifiers: LCCN 2018015761 | ISBN 9781580935128 (hardback)
Subjects: LCSH: Drawing--Technique. | BISAC: ART / Techniques / Drawing. |
ART / Techniques / Pencil Drawing. | ART / Techniques / Pen & Ink Drawing.
Classification: LCC NC730 .A675 2018 | DDC 741.2--dc23
LC record available at https://lccn.loc.gov/2018015761

ISBN 978-1-58093-512-8

Printed in China

Design and Cover Design by Jennifer K. Beal Davis
Cover illustrations by Julio Reyes (front) and Royal Charles Steadman (back)

Monacelli
A Phaidon Company
111 Broadway
New York, NY 10006

Phaidon Press Limited
2 Cooperage Yard
London E15 2QR

Phaidon SARL
55, rue Traversière
75012 Paris

phaidon.com/monacelli

CREDITS

Page 1: Ellen Isham Schutt, *Red Blackberries*, 1908, lithograph, 9 ⅘ x 6 ⁷⁄₁₀ inches (25 x 17 cm), U.S. Department of Agriculture Pomological Watercolor Collection, Rare and Special Collections, National Agricultural Library

Page 2: Julio Reyes, *Kite Flyer* (detail), 2010, graphite on paper, 23 x 20 inches (58.4 x 50.8 cm), private collection

Page 5: Royal Charles Steadman, *Malus domestica* [*Apple*], 1919, watercolor, 6 ⁷⁄₁₀ x 9 ⅘ inches (17 x 25 cm), U.S. Department of Agriculture Pomological Watercolor Collection, Rare and Special Collections, National Agricultural Library

Page 6: Susan Byron, *Rural Road 6*, 2016, charcoal, carbon, and pastel on Arches cotton paper, 4 x 4 inches (10.16 x 10.16 cm), Carrie Haddad Gallery

Calligraphy on pages 18–19 by Ellen Sontra

Illustrations on pages 70, 71, and 73 by Danika Wright

To Jeremy and Yael

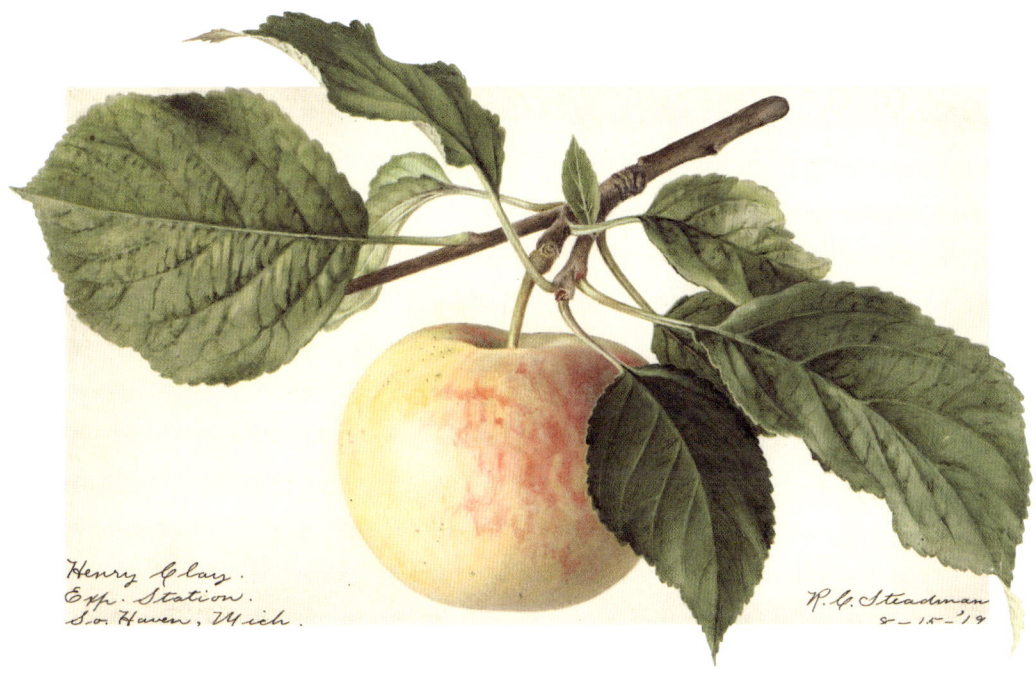

Henry Clay.
Exp. Station.
So. Haven, Mich.

R. G. Steadman
8-15-'18

Beginning my studies the first step pleas'd me so much,
The mere fact consciousness, these forms, the power of motion,
The least insect or animal, the senses, eyesight, love,
The first step I say awed me and pleas'd me so much,
I have hardly gone and hardly wish'd to go any farther,
But stop and loiter all the time to sing it in ecstatic songs.

—WALT WHITMAN, *LEAVES OF GRASS*

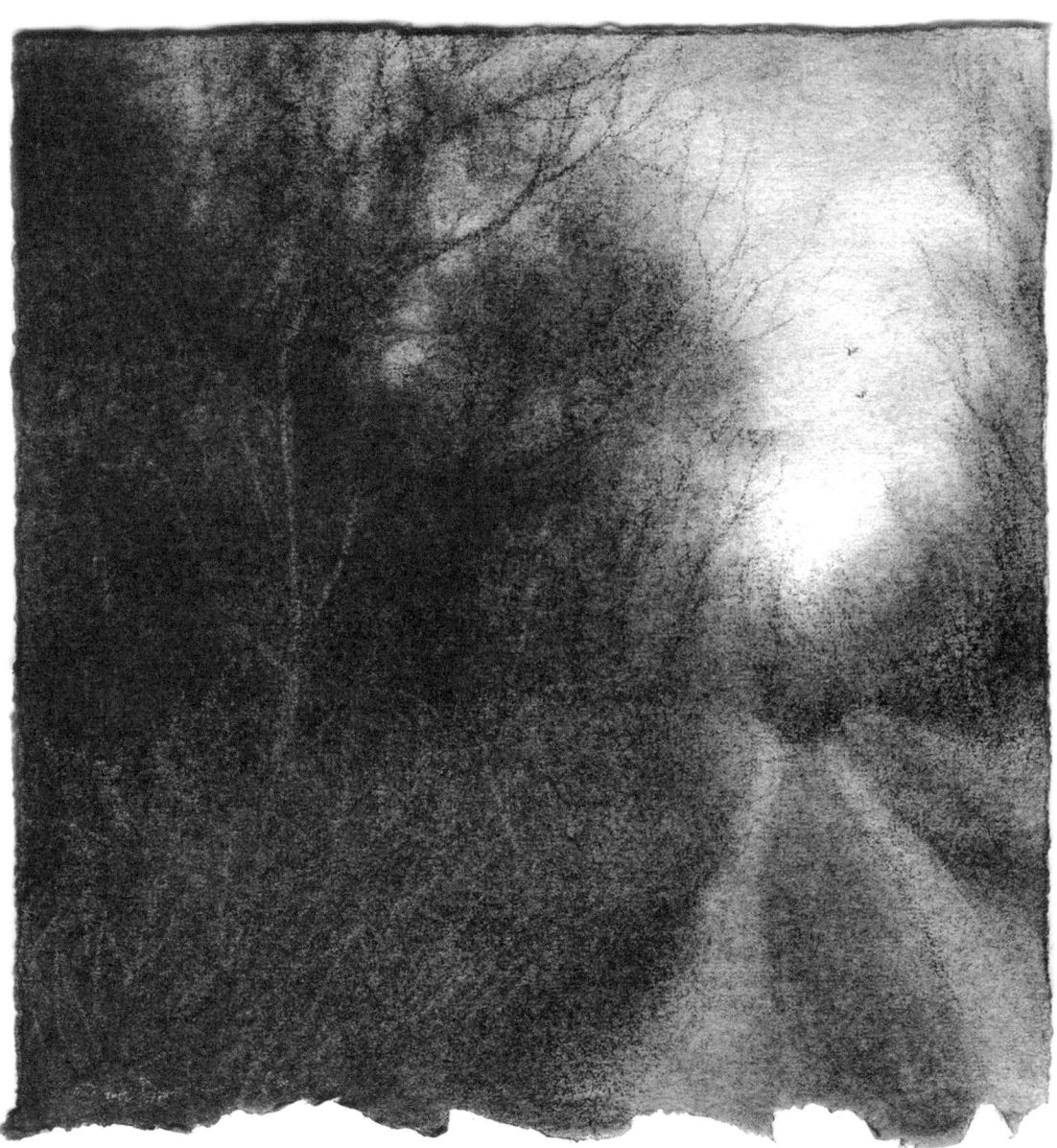

CONTENTS

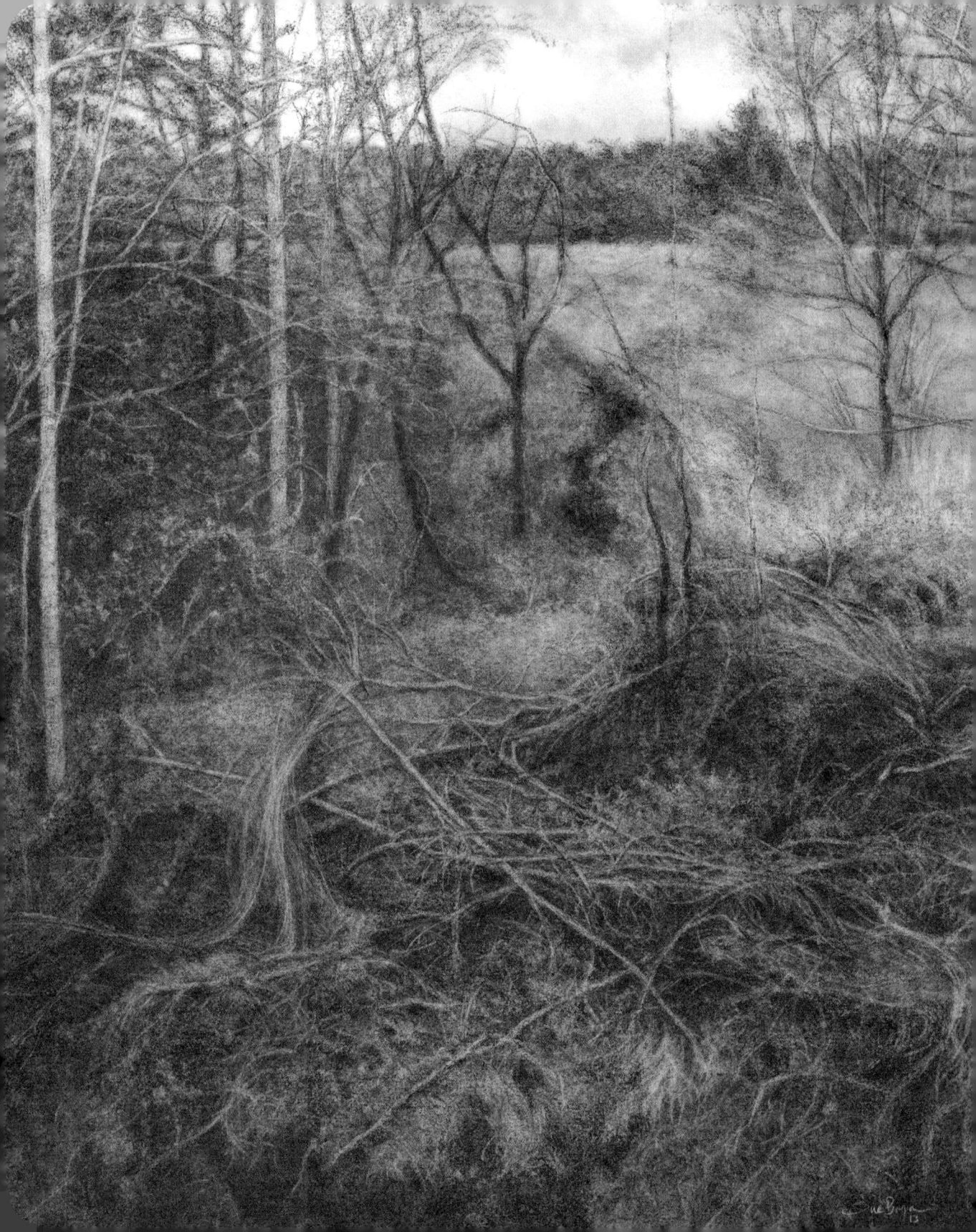

OPENING

*The beginning of our happiness lies in the
understanding that life without wonder is not worth living.*
—ABRAHAM JOSHUA HESCHEL

As a teenager, I periodically crept from my home at night, the house silent as my family slept, to walk the neighborhood and woods. Sometimes I sat with dangling legs on the small bridge leading to a tiny island on the lake, a briar pipe tasting of bitter wood between my teeth, enjoying the dark solitude. My shadow projected by moonlight onto the water, the thrill of a world asleep, the sky a trembling ceiling of a great cathedral. On my walks, I would often sketch the silhouettes of the trees: a sheet of black against a silver sky, the occasional home glowing like a lighthouse. Sometimes I would stay up all night and catch the bus to school in the morning. I didn't know it then, but I was part of the great tradition of contemplation.

There are many people who, for a time, pivot from the world to discover the shape of themselves, to learn their own minds and what makes them feel alive. They enter an empty room with a book, turn their faces to the woods, or crawl under a blanket armed with notebook and pen. Occasionally these sojourners, by withdrawing from the world, find a universe.

It was drawing that first submerged me in my thoughts and impressions, both sequestering me from the world and connecting me to my surroundings in equal measure. I found art an exhilarating source of meaning and a path that, once started, I never left. I went on to study drawing for many years with wonderful teachers who helped me build my skills and understanding. Now I share what I learned, after decades of drawing, in an atelier (artist's studio) in Seattle.

When I was a student, learning to draw was also referred to as "learning to see," because the pencil is considered an extension of the mind, which gets sharpened and challenged. The initial goal of drawing may be to capture a subject's likeness with a pencil, but more significant is our ability to become better observers. We join the ranks of the people who,

OPPOSITE: Susan Byron, *Lay of the Land*, 2013, charcoal and carbon on Arches paper, 22 ½ x 19 ½ inches (57.15 x 49.53 cm), Manifest Gallery

past the age of childhood, consider the world a strange thing worthy of examination. People who stand amazed at the improbability of the everyday are often known as artists, poets, and writers, but perhaps they are just like the rest of us, the only difference being that they have chosen to make careers of their wonder.

Drawing allows each of us to become a visual philosopher, questioning what we see, exploring uncertainty, and seeking beauty. We are not waiting on the sidelines as life flows by unexamined. Through drawing we develop the deep appreciation that comes from careful looking, and we learn that there is nothing ordinary in life. Any place can be the source of beauty and the subject of great art.

You may have thought that only some people can draw well and others cannot, that some are talented and you are not. This is simply not true. If you can write a letter, you can learn to draw. In grade school, you learned the precision of lines that form letters, the curves and spacing of each word, the proportion of the various letters. If you can't write it's not because you lack capacity, but because you were not taught. The ability to draw lives in you as much as it does in any artist; in fact, it is your right. The journey of learning to draw contains some risk. There may be a feeling of clumsiness or foolishness as you start, and you may get a little lost, but there is a great reward at the end. Drawing is a slow art: it takes time. Your growth, both in sight and insight, will be proportional to the amount of time you spend at it. Yet even a minimal investment of time will give you some artistic skill that can inform how you see.

This book is for people of all ages who aspire to train their eyes and hands. This is a remarkably diverse group. My workshops are attended not only by art students, but also doctors, nurses, executives, tech workers, hair stylists, chefs, teachers, and professionals from every imaginable industry. They come to learn how to think like artists—to gain aesthetic insight—because to see more clearly is to think more clearly. This book is also for people who want to record their observations, travels, and experiences.

In the process of learning about art, you will begin to experience your life and environment more deeply as a world that is uniquely yours. Only *you* see through your eyes. You have something to say that no one else can. You deserve to express what is inside you, so let's pick up a pencil and get started.

OPPOSITE: Julio Reyes, *Nothing Gold Can Stay*, 2016, graphite on paper, 23 x 20 inches (40 x 35.3 cm), private collection

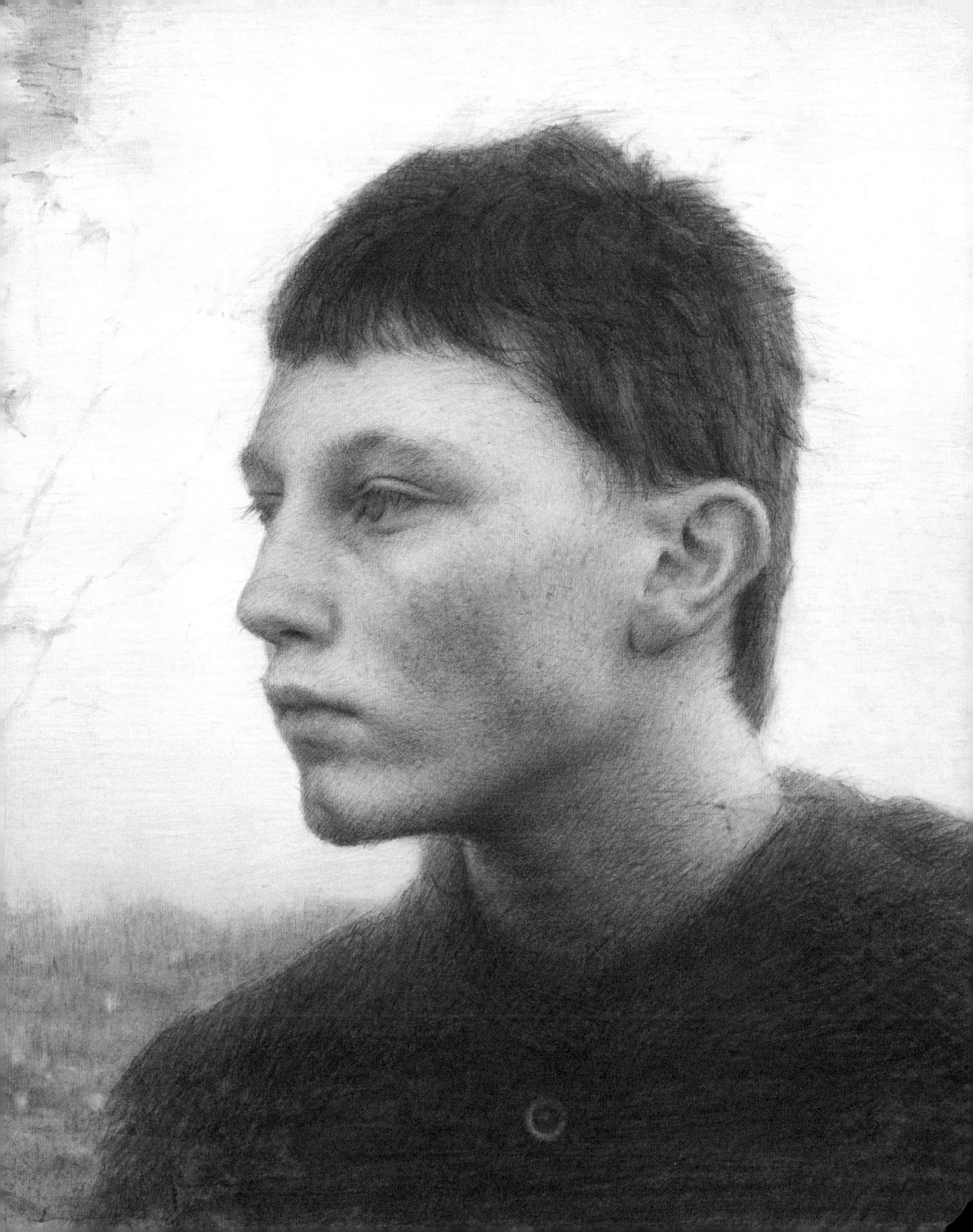

Before we begin

This sketchbook is meant to be used, written on, and sketched in. The best way to learn about art is by making it. Learning, not perfection, is the goal, so get your hands dirty and risk ruining this book as you draw in it.

Here are a few tips to keep in mind as you work through the book:

- When following a step-by-step progression, draw your steps on top of each other, letting each stage absorb the previous one. Alternatively, you can just practice whichever stage of the drawing you feel most comfortable with.

- Draw lightly. Start with a hard pencil, which makes lighter marks that are easier to erase if you have a false start. Practice using a dull, soft pencil for the calligraphy page to get the variation in line weight. (For more about pencils, see below.)

- When starting a drawing, place a few rough lines rather than trying to get one perfect starting line. False starts and errant lines can be erased later.

- Don't try to make the blackest areas of the drawing directly. Use your graphite to build up values gradually and softly, even in your darkest areas.

- Go slowly to get the best results. We see things when we slow down that we don't notice at high speeds. You don't have to finish a drawing in one sitting. Put the sketchbook aside when you are tired, and come back later to finish.

- Making and finding mistakes is not a problem; it is an important part of the process. However, not wanting to make—or find—a mistake *is* a problem that will ultimately delay your progress.

Materials

The only materials you need for this book are a pencil, an eraser, and a pencil sharpener. For drawings with color, you can use colored pencils in sepia or umber.

Any pencil can be used, even in a pinch the classic yellow schoolhouse #2 (which translates to an HB). I prefer to start with a medium graphite pencil, such as an H (or HB), which can be pushed quite dark before switching to a softer pencil to get even darker. When buying a pencil at the art store, look at the stamp at the end of the pencil. "H" stands for "hardness" and "B" for "blackness"; the higher the number, the harder (and lighter) or softer (and darker) it is. Mechanical pencils are a good choice, too, and they are easy to keep sharp.

The pink erasers on the ends of pencils can damage the page, so go lightly, or consider getting a good hard white polymer eraser or a kneaded eraser.

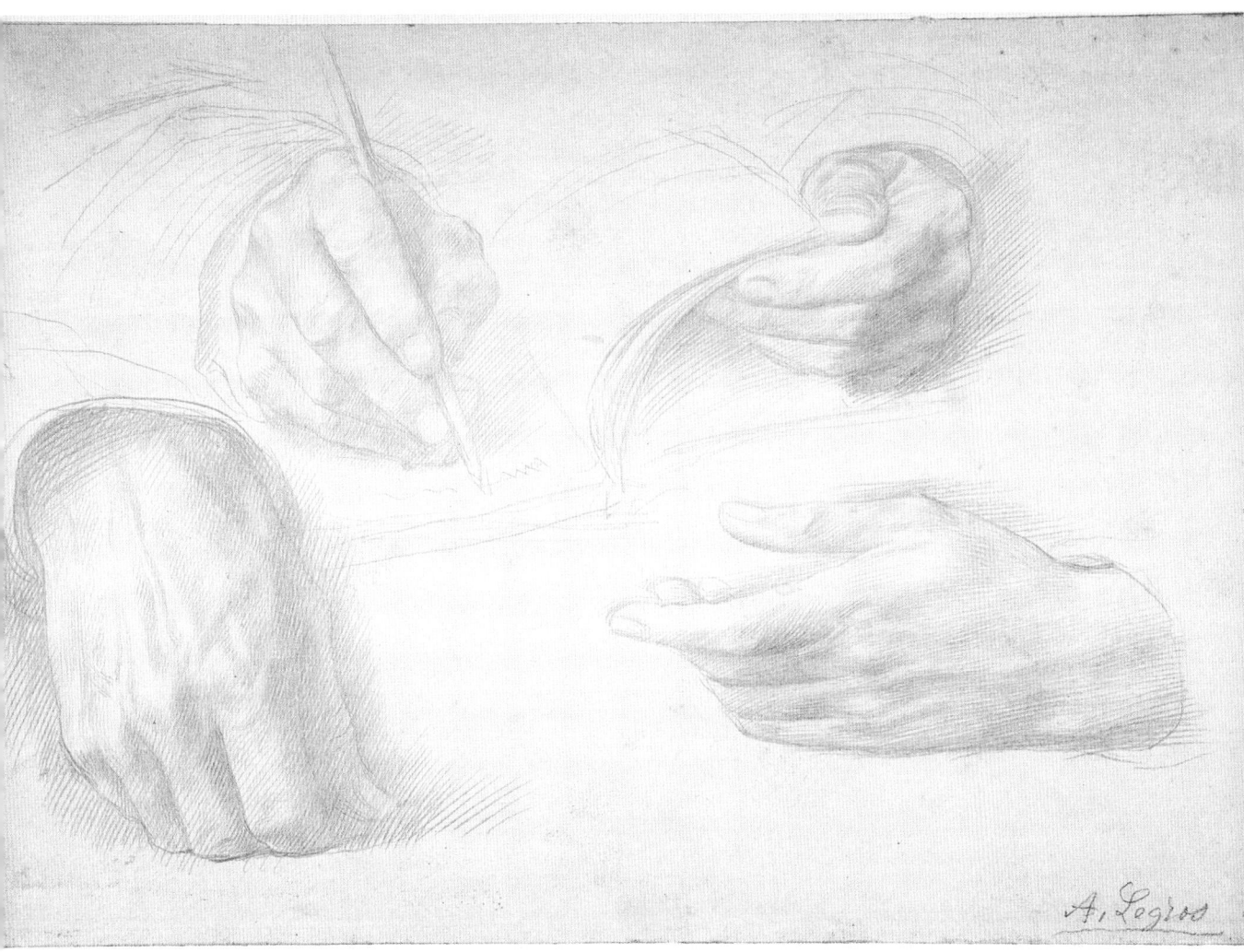

On the practice of "mastercopy"

This book is based on the principle that copying master drawings is one of the best ways to improve your work. We learn to speak and gain social graces and basic life skills before we are old enough to remember exactly how it all began. While growing up, I learned to cook almost by osmosis just by being around my mom, who made dinner every night. We learn many things through example that are hard to learn otherwise. This process of learning through emulation, which serves us so well in life, also once formed the basis of art training,

ABOVE: Alphonse Legros, *Study of Hands*, date unknown, metalpoint on prepared paper, 9 ³⁄₁₆ x 13 ¼ inches (23.4 x 33.7 cm), Metropolitan Museum of Art (gift of the artist, 1892)

with students starting as assistants in workshops. When art academies were founded, students began by copying drawings, sculptures, and plaster casts, and only then drew live models.

This progression of study—first copying works of art and only later creating original pieces—resulted in some of the finest works of art ever made. And so, the history of art education in the Western world is entwined with the practice of copying masterpieces, called "mastercopy."

Mastercopy was such an important part of Renaissance art training that the list of practitioners is a "who's who" of art history. Luminaries such as Leonardo da Vinci, Raphael, and Michelangelo extensively studied Greco-Roman sculptures to learn the delicate balance of naturalism and idealism, revitalizing the art of their day. This practice was not just for artists in the early stages of learning; for some, it was a lifelong study. As Eugène Delacroix wrote about his hero, Peter Paul Rubens, in his journal: "Rubens was more than fifty years old when he was sent on a mission to the King of Spain, yet he spent his free time in copying the superb Italian originals that can still be seen in Madrid. In his youth, he did an enormous amount of copying. This practice… was the source of his immense knowledge."

In the nineteenth century, drawing courses supplied in books became popular ways for students to follow along and gain artistic skills. Vincent van Gogh wrote to his brother about copying plates from one such book, *Cours de dessin* (*Drawing course*), by Charles Bargue and Jean-Léon Gérôme: "Careful study and the constant and repeated copying of Bargue's exercises have given me an insight into figure drawing. I have learned to measure and to see and to look for the broad outlines, so that, thank God, what seemed utterly impossible to me before is gradually becoming possible now. I no longer stand as helpless before nature as I used to do." Now reprinted as *Charles Bargue: Drawing Course,* Bargue's book is still a great resource used to train artists today.

The ultimate goal of these exercises was not servile imitation but the freedom that comes with mastering a skill set. *Beginning Drawing Atelier* is built upon this premise, that we learn best through example, so follow along in this historic discipline of mastercopy and see how it improves your drawing skills. Later, you will be able to channel the lessons to draw whatever most inspires you.

OPPOSITE: Charles Bargue, Plate I, 23: *Man's arm bent (Bras d'homme, ployé, extérieur)*, lithograph from *Cours de dessin* (Paris: Goupil & Cie, 1866). Image courtesy of Art Renewal Center

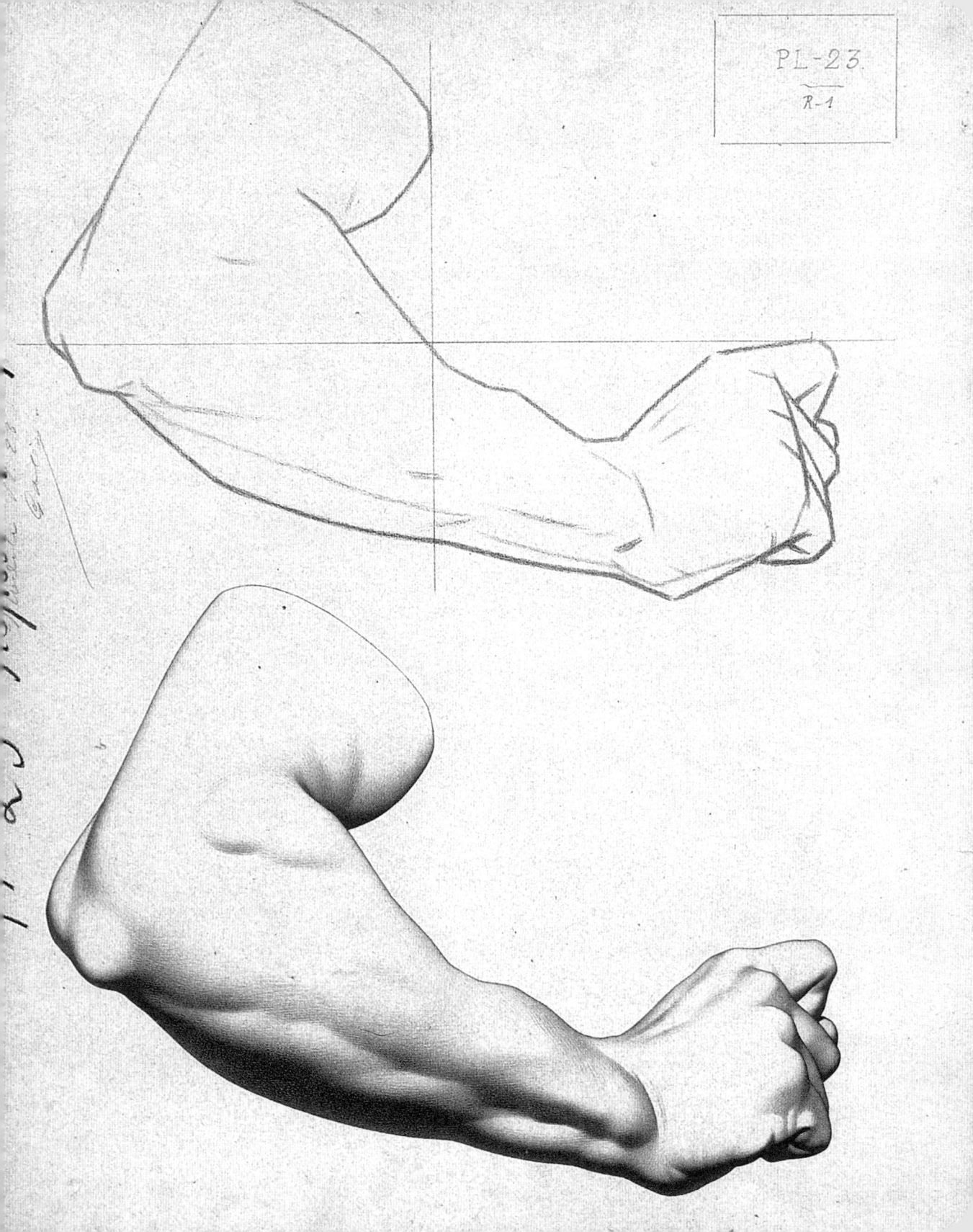

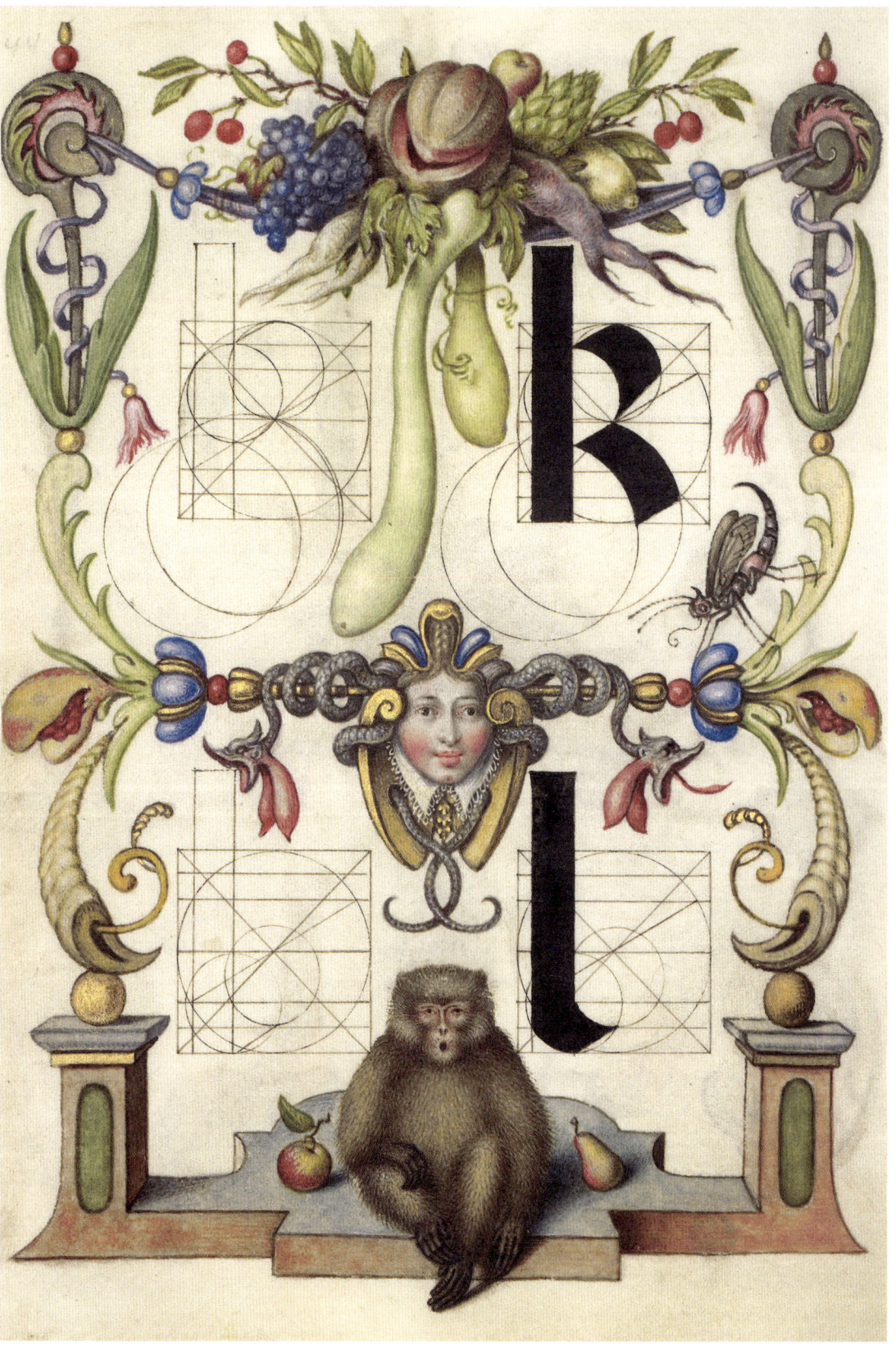

ONE

LINE

*It was the habit of Apelles not to allow a day to be so full that
he had no time to practice his art by drawing a line.*

PLINY THE ELDER, *NATURAL HISTORY*

We start at the beginning: the line itself.

When you sign your name at the end of a letter, the writing is forceful and clear. It isn't shaky and scratchy, because you are working with purpose. Your mind and hand know what to do. Yet none of us start life knowing how to write; it is a skill acquired over time, requiring both instruction and practice. The building blocks of drawing are no different from those of learning the letters of the alphabet. I remember practicing letters over and over to get uniform sizes and spacing, neatness, and control. I remember my frustrated parents wondering if I would ever get the hang of it. Now, of course, penmanship comes without thinking. The same potential exists in drawing. Confidence comes on the far side of instruction and practice; everyone who can write his or her name has the capacity.

In this chapter we aim to draw strong lines and understand how line direction can be used as a compositional device. A straight line is a directional force, propelling our vision from one area to another. It has movement, much as if it had an arrow at the tip pointing your eye ahead. We'll start by practicing lines for their own sake, then explore how great draftsmen of the past used a few key lines to create rhythm in their drawings. These repeating, or governing, lines constitute a hidden design in many artworks, almost like a refrain in music, creating harmony and a sense of a unified purpose. As the twentieth-century artist Jacques Villon—also known as Gaston Duchamp—said, "The framework of a work of art is also its most secret and deepest poetry."

OPPOSITE: Joris Hoefnagel, *Guide for Constructing the Letters k and l*, ca. 1591–96, watercolor, gold and silver paint, and ink on parchment, 6 9/16 x 4 7/8 inches (16.7 x 12.4 cm), J. Paul Getty Museum

DRAW LETTERS

Some early American drawing books taught handwriting along with drawing. The same lines used for letters are also used for drawing pictures. Use a soft, dull pencil to re-create these lines and letterforms by Ellen Sontra. Press hard for the downstroke and light for the upstroke to get a real difference in line thickness. Go slowly and steadily. Great letters are made with deliberation.

Lines form letters and drawings

Practice:

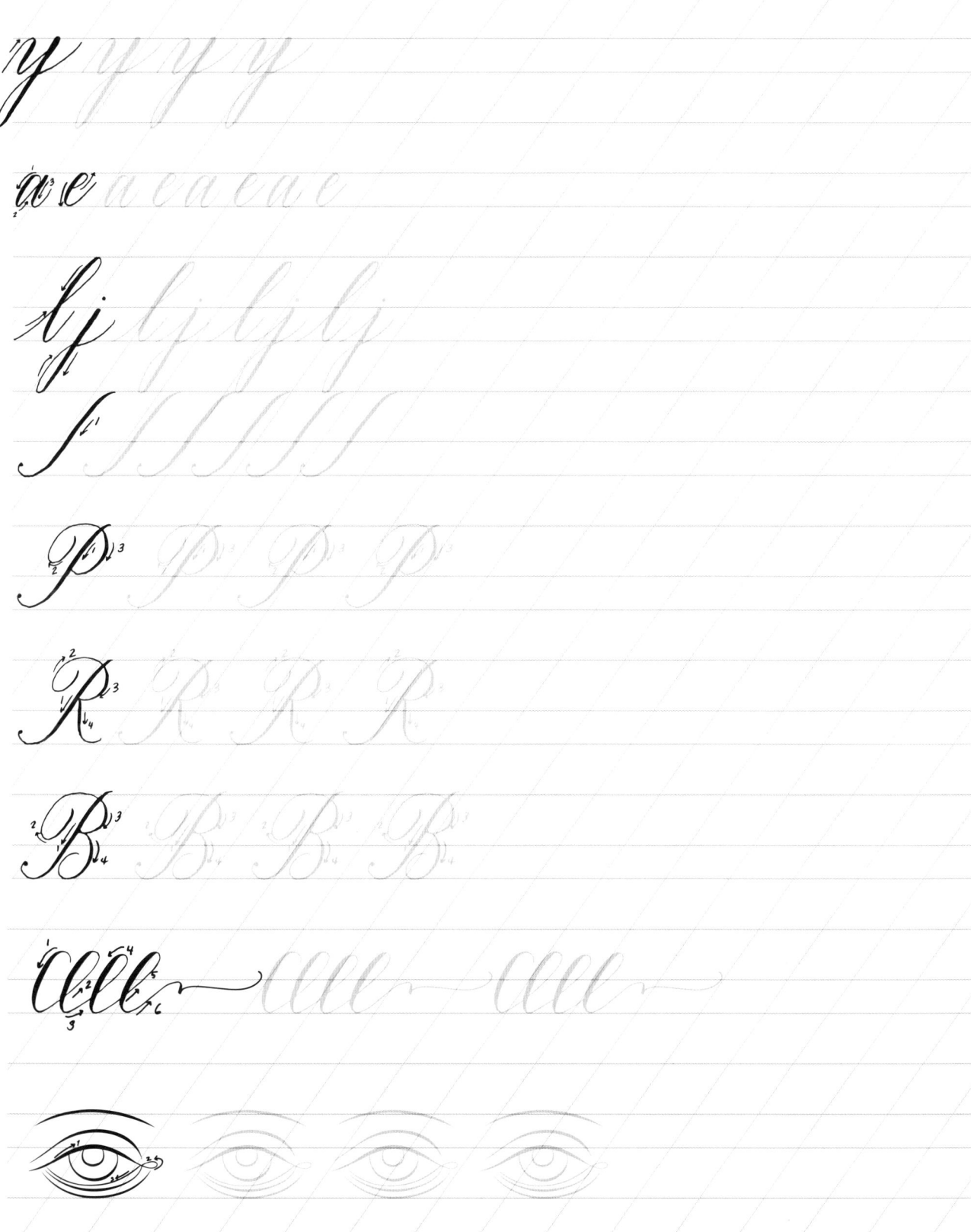

DRAW LINES

Just as when practicing your ABCs, we start with simple line directions without worrying about forming words right away. Be goal oriented: when placing a line, determine where you want the line to end (rather than focusing on the tip of your pencil) and move there directly with intention.

Place the tip of your pencil on a dot and draw a line down to its partner dot. Feel how confidently your pencil moves from dot to dot. This is how you should feel when working on your drawings. Multiple thin lines—placed lightly, with the confidence of knowing any line can be adjusted later—are better than a thick, trembly line anxiously drawn. Keep your lines light so they erase easily. Don't be discouraged if this task is harder than it looks; do the exercise without judging your efforts.

Let your line start forcefully, then allow it to get lighter, fading gradually as it slides over the end dot. Trust that the line is correct and don't second-guess it. Practice making a range of assertive lines: verticals, horizontals, and semicircles.

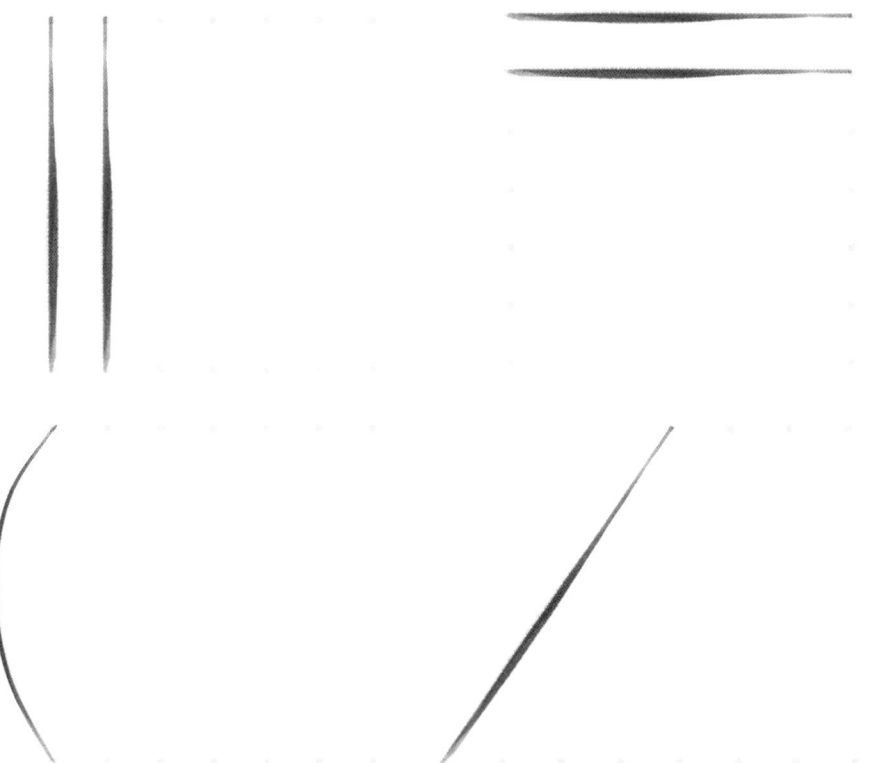

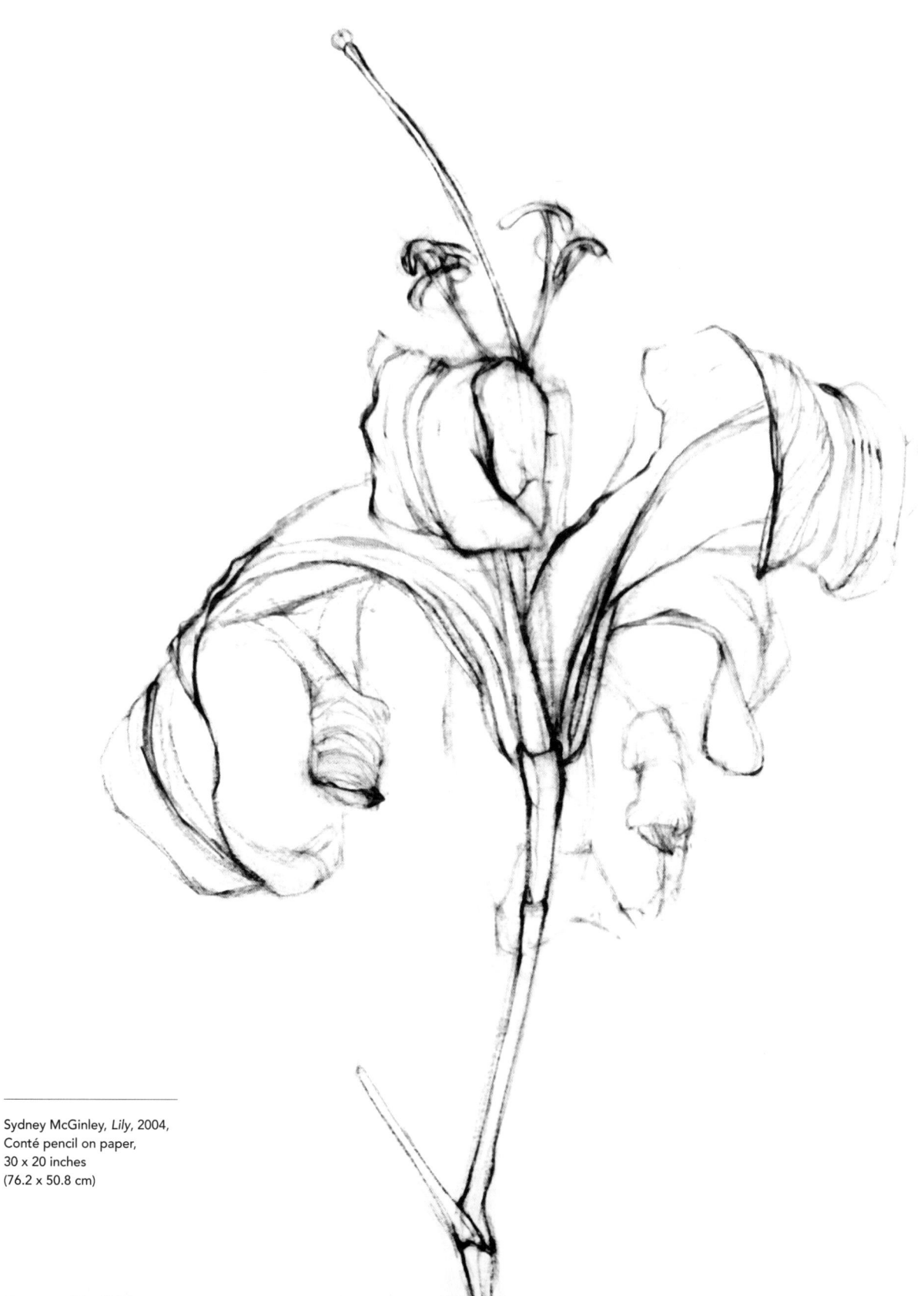

Sydney McGinley, *Lily*, 2004,
Conté pencil on paper,
30 x 20 inches
(76.2 x 50.8 cm)

Finding design through governing lines

A great drawing always starts with an emotional response to your subject. Look past the details and likeness and, instead, focus on your subject's hidden essential patterns and structure. Often, this is no more than a single repeating line direction, or just a few dynamic angles, but the result is like a storyline that summarizes a whole book. You can lightly draw these lines in your image as you begin, or just keep them in your mind, allowing them to subtly influence your drawing as it develops.

FIND GOVERNING LINES

Most master drawings have a theme built on simple lines. In the subsequent drawings, we are going to find the role of vertical, horizontal, and diagonal lines.

First, draw directly over the John Ruskin drawing, opposite, to see how many vertical lines you can find. Make your lines long, running each line past where you see it start and end. Next, look for horizontal lines. Draw them across the page—big lines, not tiny dashes—to see what else each one hits. Lastly, do you see any semicircles? Are you surprised how much of this complex-looking drawing was created by only three line directions?

OPPOSITE: John Ruskin, *The Pulpit in the Church of S. Ambrogio*, 19th century, watercolor on paper, 17 ⅛ x 13 inches (43.8 x 33 cm), Victoria and Albert Museum. Image courtesy of Art Renewal Center

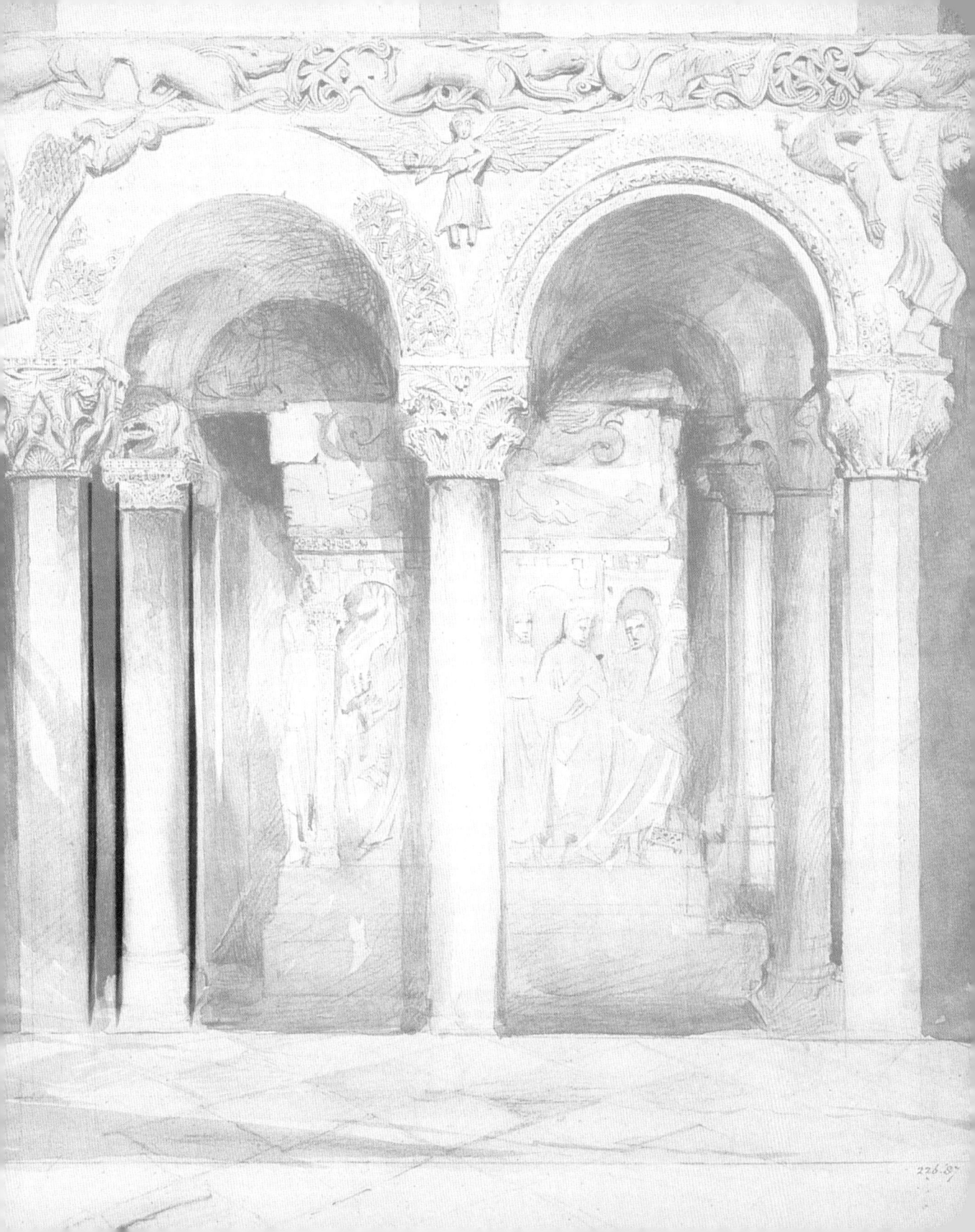

226.⊗

Line directions are letters in the draftsperson's alphabet. When one direction is emphasized or used in combination with others, rhythm and design are created. The diagonal line conveys motion and instability; its movement defies the pull of gravity. Théodore Géricault chose the diagonal to use throughout his drawing, shown opposite, to express the dynamic force of horses in motion.

In his book *Art and Visual Perception,* Rudolf Arnheim, a perceptual psychologist working in the twentieth century, asked us to consider a line as directed tension. "Think of a rope that is motionless while two men of equal strength are pulling it in opposite directions," he wrote. "It is still, but loaded with energy." A confident diagonal line conveys this tension, like a tightly pulled rubber band ready to release.

Practice drawing diagonal lines below, connecting the dots as shown. Let your pencil rest on the first point before aiming for the second. Then, sketch as many repeating diagonal lines as you can find on the slightly faded, ghosted version of Géricault's horses, opposite. Wherever you see a line, draw it long to see how it informs the drawing.

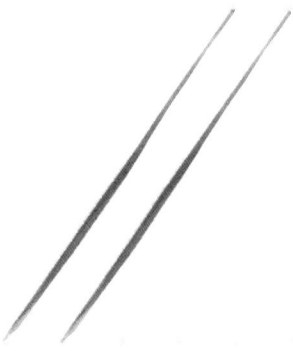

OPPOSITE: Théodore Géricault, *Horses and Riders*, 1813–14, graphite on paper, 8¼ × 11 inches (21 × 27.9 cm), J. Paul Getty Museum

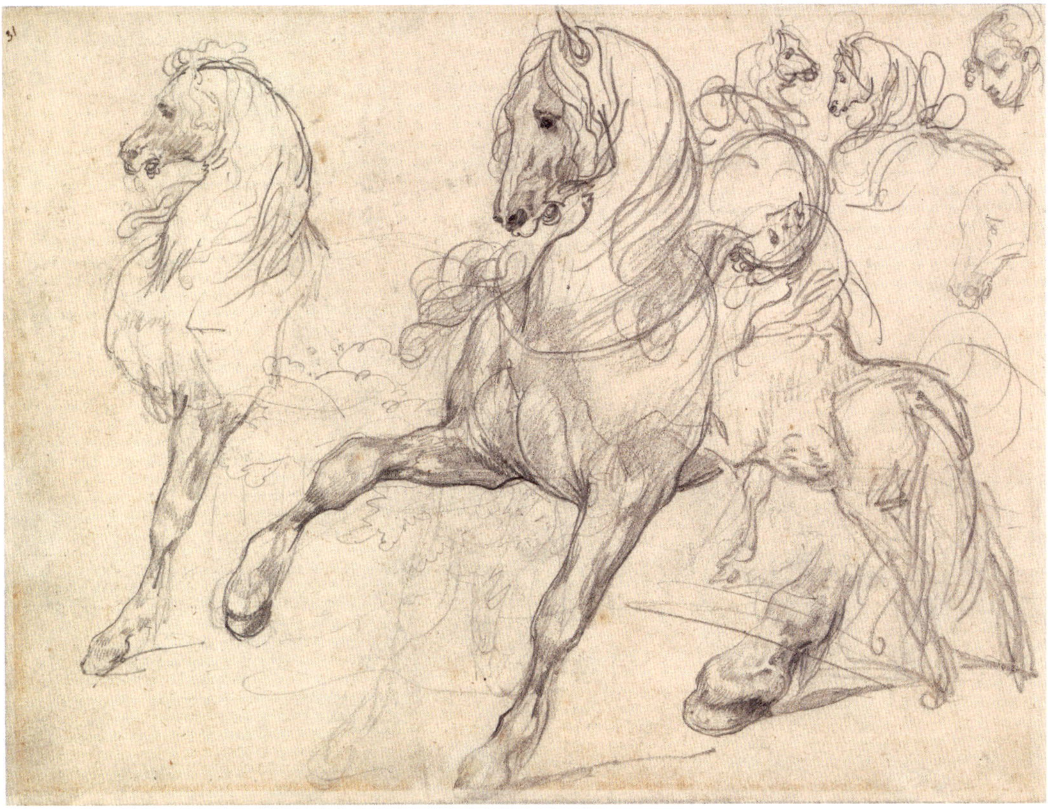
31

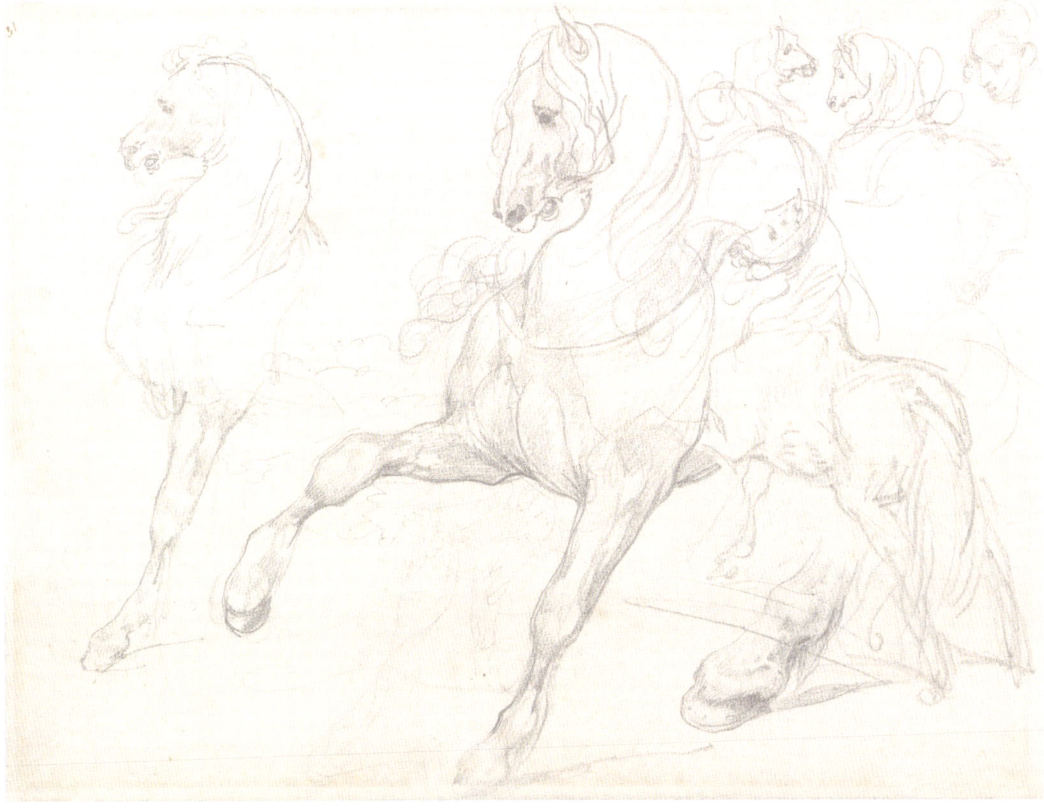
31

Practice drawing curved lines below, connecting the dots as shown. Then, in the Kenyon Cox drawing, opposite, look for the big sweeping "C." This graceful line connects diverse elements of the piece, bringing unity to a drawing that might otherwise feel fragmented. Sketch on top of the ghosted version wherever you see this line of movement.

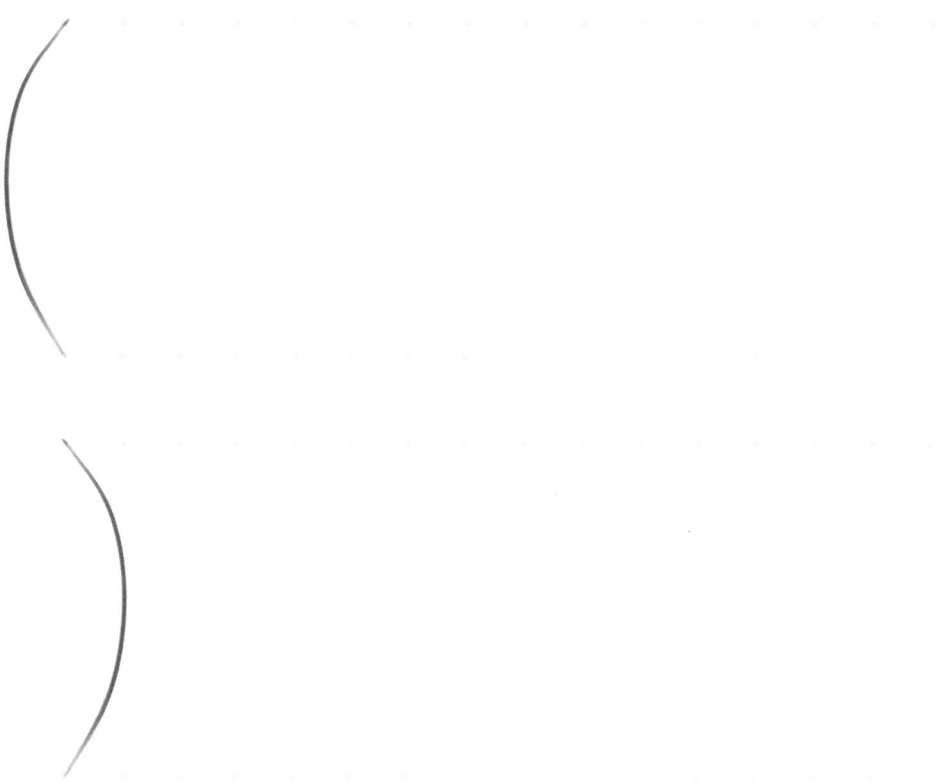

OPPOSITE: Kenyon Cox, *Drapery Study for the Figure of Physics*, 1896, graphite and ink on paper, size unknown, Library of Congress

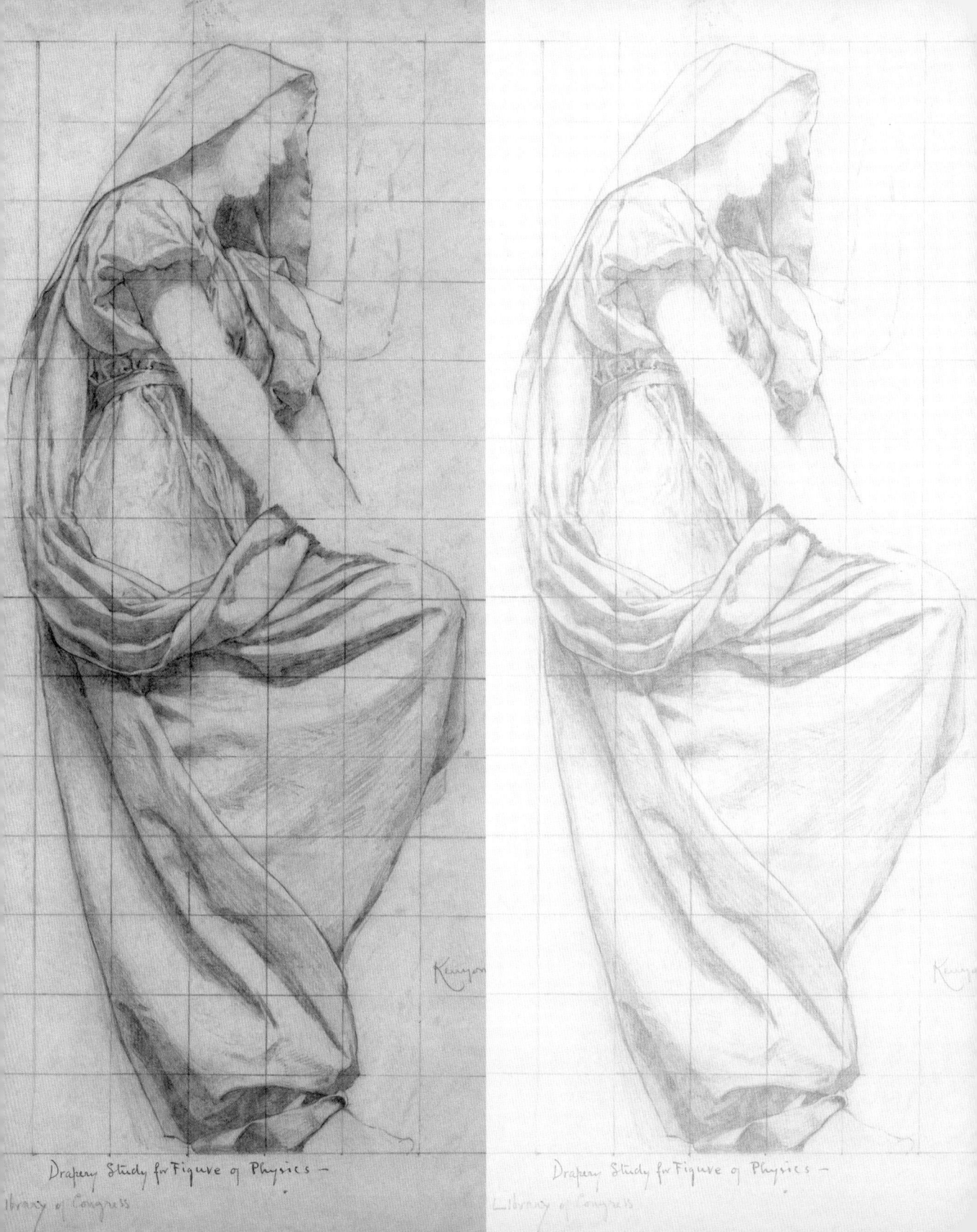

Drapery Study for Figure of Physics —
Library of Congress

Drapery Study for Figure of Physics —
Library of Congress

Using Adolf von Menzel's drawing of rooftops, below, sketch as many repeating diagonal, vertical, and horizontal lines as you can find. See how artists play with a few line directions to create repetition and complexity.

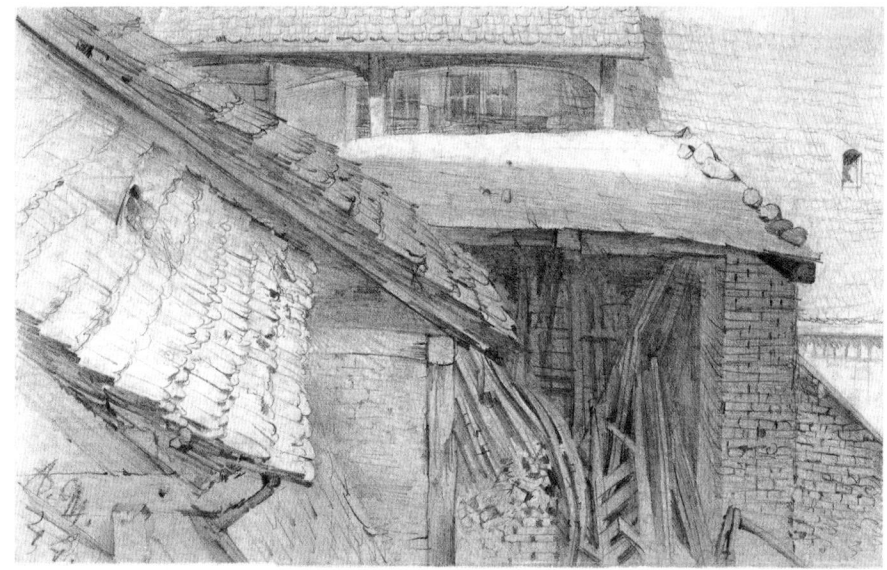

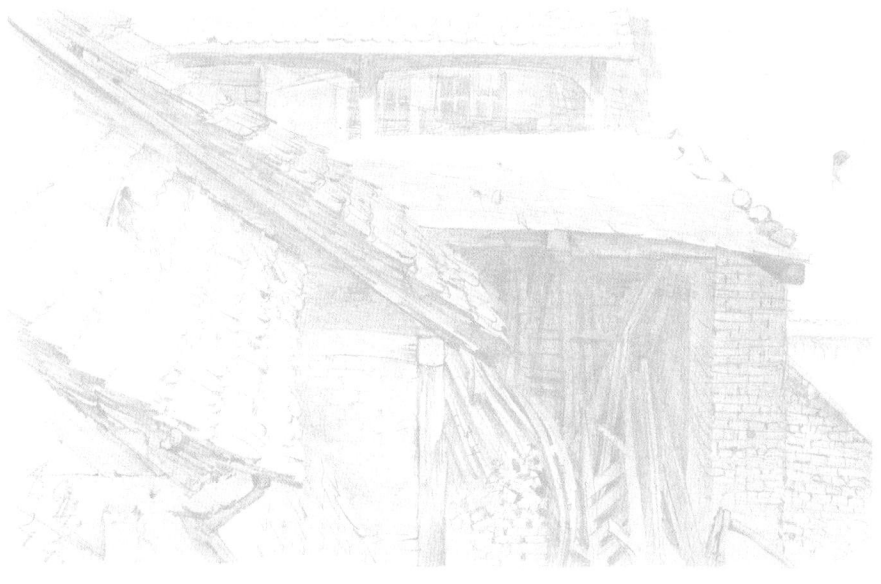

Adolph von Menzel, *Back Yard of the Puhlmann House near Potsdam*, 1844, graphite on paper, 4 ⁹⁄₁₀ x 8 inches (12.5 x 20.5 cm), bpk Bildagentur/Art Resource, NY

We do not, or need not, despair of drawing because all lines must be either curved or straight, nor of painting because there are only three "primary" colours. We may indeed be older now, in so far as we are heirs in enjoyment or in practice of many generations of ancestors in the arts. In this inheritance of wealth there may be a danger of boredom or of anxiety to be original, and that may lead to a distaste for fine drawing, delicate pattern, and "pretty" colours.... But the true road of escape from such weariness is not to be found in the wilfully awkward, clumsy, or misshapen.... Before we reach such states we need recovery.

—J.R.R. TOLKIEN, *ON FAIRY STORIES*

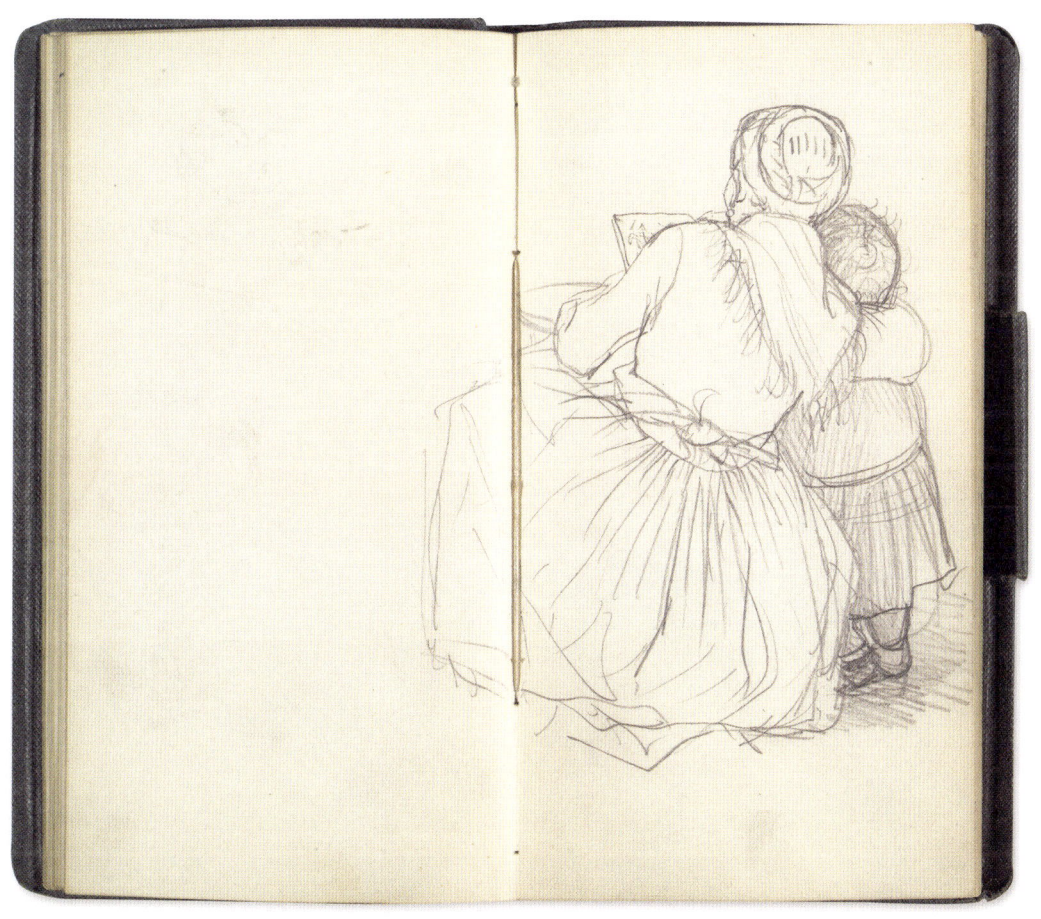

Adolf von Menzel, *Sketchbook*, 1863, pencil on paper, size unknown, J. Paul Getty Museum

In the drawing below, Leonardo da Vinci explores proportions and relationships within the human head. These lines are not random; da Vinci mapped a web of connections made by vertical, horizontal, and diagonal lines. Lightly trace each line, noticing all the elements connected along its course. The fewer angles used, the more unified and compelling the portrait. The practice of limiting your line directions is not only good design; it also allows the artist to cross-check for accuracy.

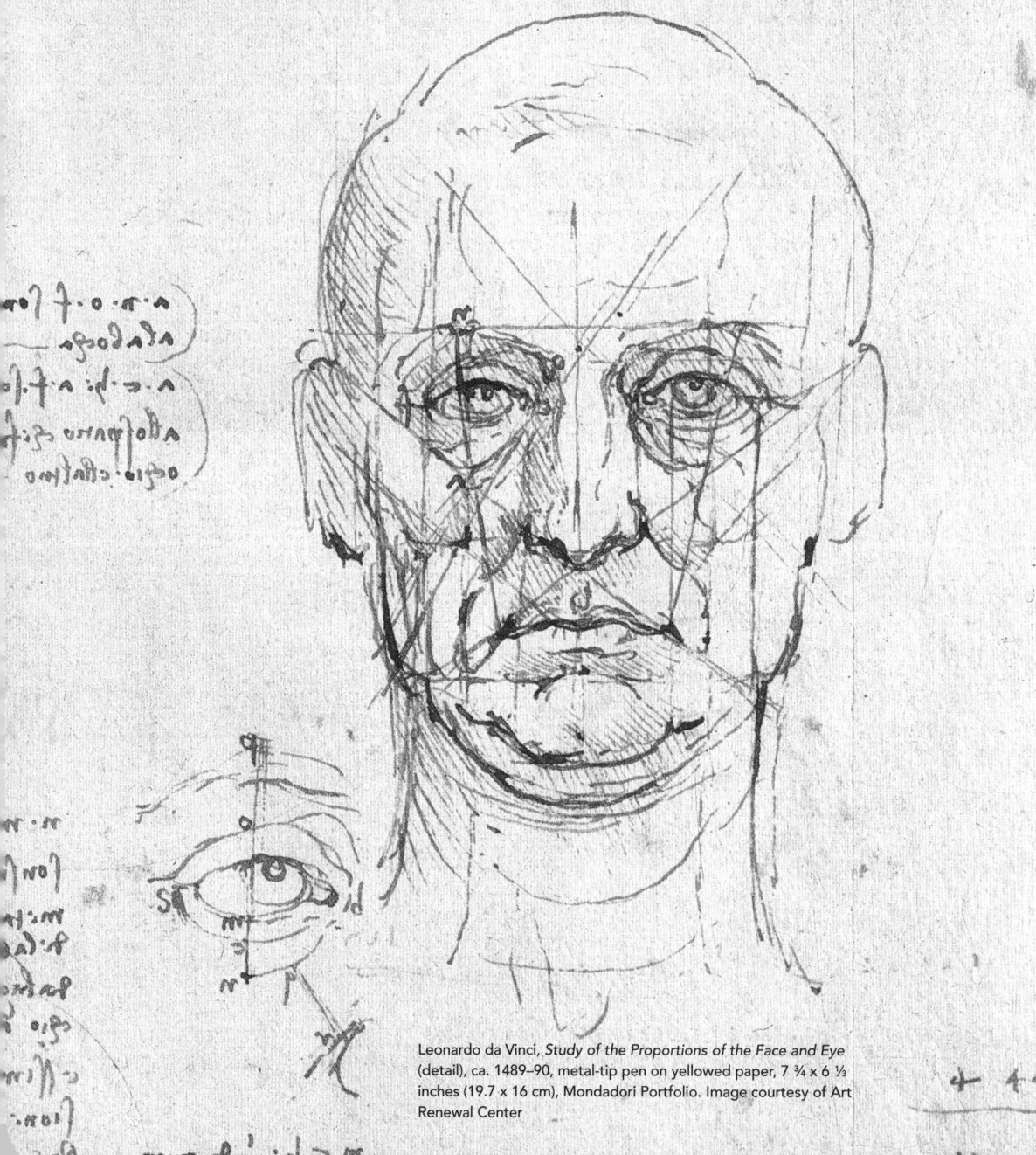

Leonardo da Vinci, *Study of the Proportions of the Face and Eye* (detail), ca. 1489–90, metal-tip pen on yellowed paper, 7 ¾ x 6 ⅓ inches (19.7 x 16 cm), Mondadori Portfolio. Image courtesy of Art Renewal Center

Re-create da Vinci's drawing by filling in this face with the missing lines. First, place the three horizontal lines across the brow and under the nose and mouth. Next, find the vertical lines, starting with the centerline of the face. Drop more vertical lines from the eyes down the face, even running a few through the neck. Lastly, find the diagonals, such as from the corner of the eyes through the nose and the corner of the mouth. When you're finished, look at the face of a friend or your own face in the mirror. Can you find similar relationships?

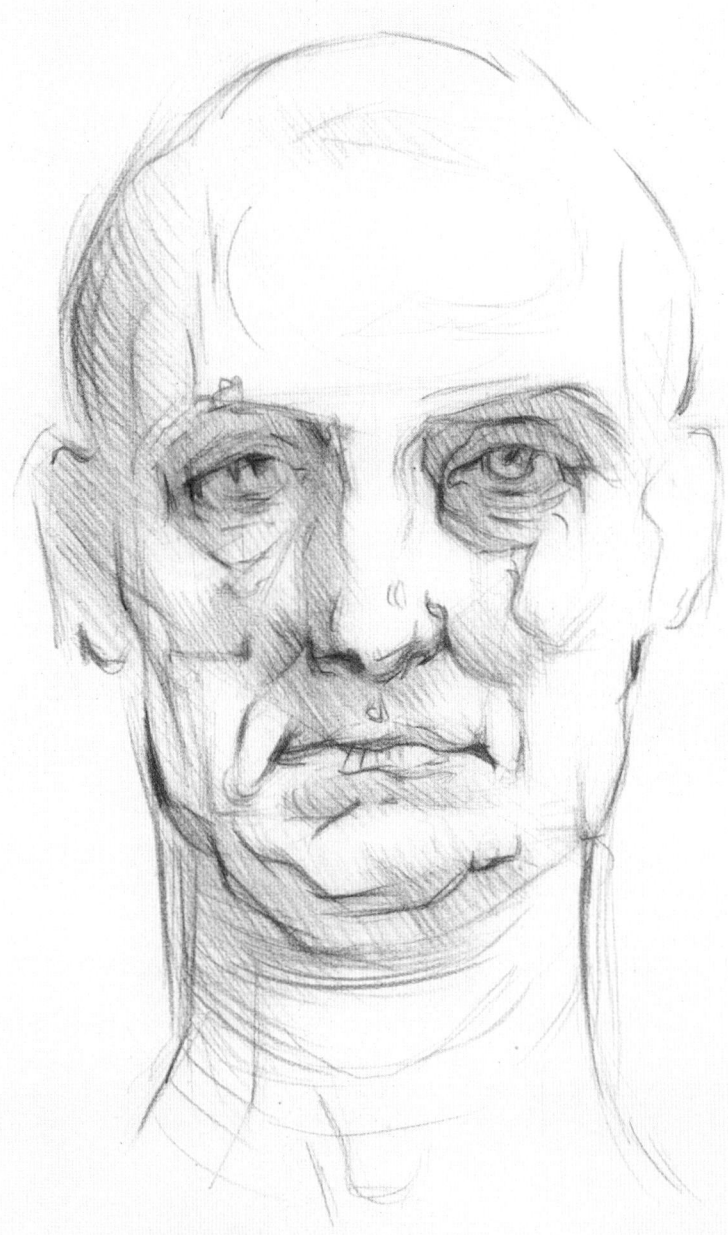

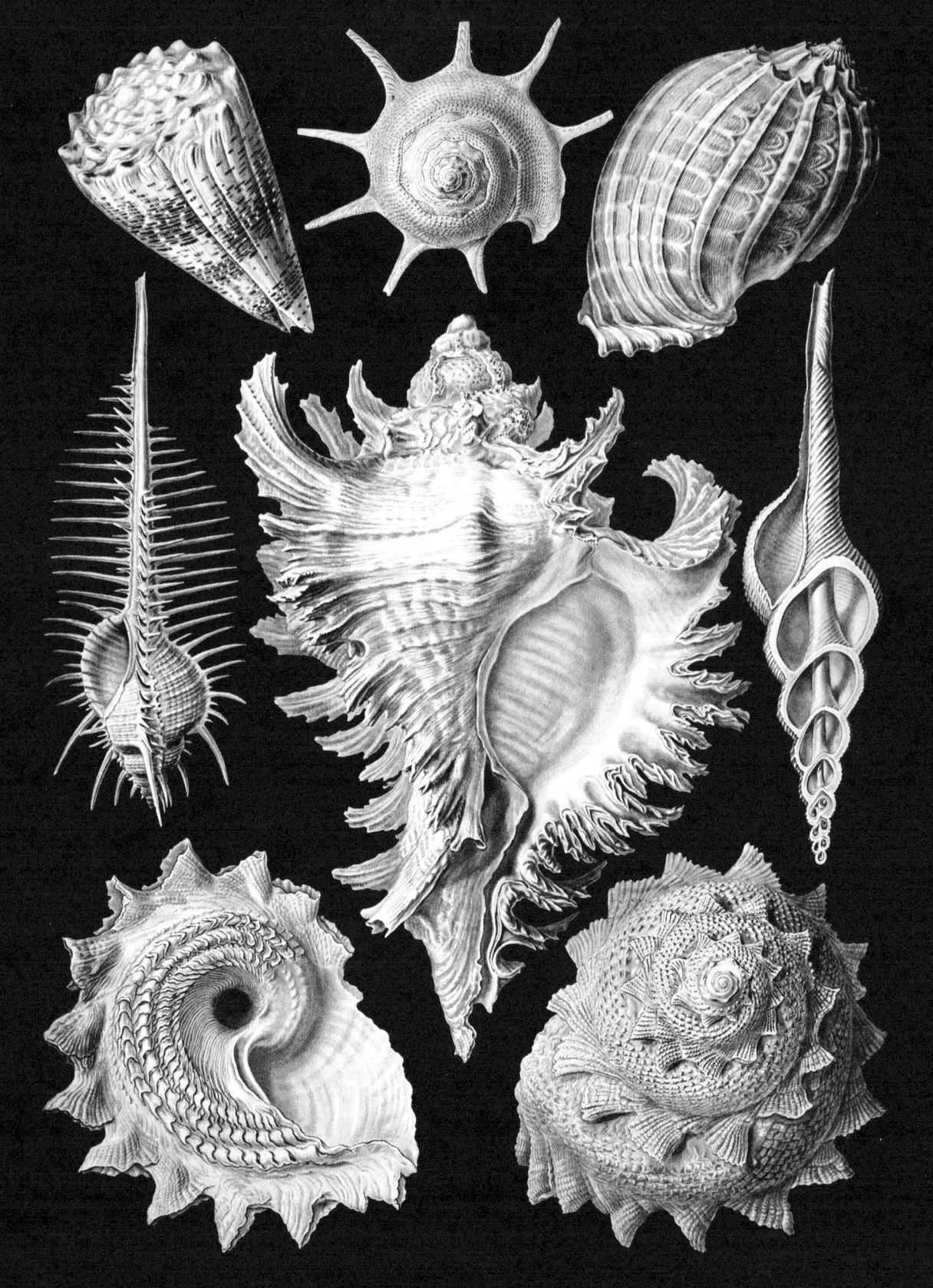

SHAPE

Looking closely at nature, the first insight we obtain is that,
behind the apparently endless proliferation of natural objects, there is a
far lesser number of apparently fixed types.
—MICHAEL S. SCHNEIDER, *A BEGINNER'S GUIDE TO CONSTRUCTING THE UNIVERSE*

We start our drawings when the tip of our pencil presses against the paper and makes a point. A line forms when we connect one point to another and move our pencil in a direction. As we place multiple lines, they join together, connecting to form a shape. In this chapter, we'll practice seeing shapes and then using them to start our drawings with a technique called *blocking in.*

I heard that the writer Bertrand Russell dictated his books so eloquently that his first thought became the final word. More common are writers like me, who roughly map a book, develop an outline, and then write increasingly refined drafts. In drawing, the likelihood of creating an image perfectly on the first try is as uncommon as writing a book without corrections. Experienced artists often work like writers, starting with a general sketch of ideas and refining them over time. And in drawing, the first step of this process is the *block-in.*

A block-in is an abstract shape that approximates our subject in a general way. A good block-in maps out the subject's scale (how big it is), where the image sits on the page, and the general proportion of width to height. It often captures a few important angle directions to establish the first, most basic, shape of our subject. As the name implies, the shapes you are left with at this stage are often blocky and simplified, yet if accurately done, you can begin to see a hint of the finished image. And as you continue to refine your block-in, checking it for accuracy and making it more and more detailed, the actual shape of your subject emerges.

OPPOSITE: Ernst Haeckel, *Prosbrachia*, lithograph, from *Kunstformen der Natur*, 1904

Learning to see shape

To start, let's take a look at how we see shape. It is common for beginning art students to fall into ways of seeing that are symbolic and imagined, rather than actually observed. To test this, sketch a leaf and a fish on a piece of scrap paper. Are you finished? When drawing these objects, you didn't need them right in front of you because your mind conjured a picture. Yet the skills that enable us to quickly link names to objects—so essential in life—are a liability in drawing. Our drawings from imagination often stand in for "any leaf" or "any fish," rather than one in particular. This type of symbolism may work well for airport signage, but not so well for capturing the beauty of nature in art.

Beginning students inadvertently bring this symbolic seeing into their drawings. They draw an outline of an eye even if part of the eye is obscured, four legs of a table even if only two are visible, or an ellipse for a cup even if the cup is seen at eye level. Objects in real life are often concealed, incomplete, and presented in unexpected views; they rarely look anything like the symbolic versions of themselves. In life, we see every variation of a fish, or a leaf, in various colors, shapes, sizes, vantage points, and kinds of light. So in order to capture objects in real life, we must break away from symbolic seeing. We must focus on an object's shape, rather than *what an object is*. Focusing on an object's name or function leads to mere symbolism, while slow observation of an object's shape leads to renewed seeing.

Balancing universal and particular shapes

Renaissance artists believed the natural world was the handiwork of God and could be mined for secrets to the universe. They, like the ancient Greeks before them, studied nature to uncover its hidden geometric underpinning and design and then used these patterns and ratios in their art and architecture.

In contrast to reducing objects to symbols, there is a long history in art of studying people, plants, and animals to understand their universal qualities. Every object has qualities that are common to its type, while also being unique. For example, each cat is unique, yet also shares traits with other cats that make them different from birds or trees. Every person's skeleton shares common markers, yet every person is individual. This is a balance of universals and particulars—between the ideal forms, which we sense, and the imperfect ones we see.

In this section, we are going to channel our inner Renaissance artist to look for simple shapes in everyday items and then adjust them into more complex realistic forms.

OPPOSITE: Katsushika Hokusai, *Insects*, 1812, woodblock print, size unknown

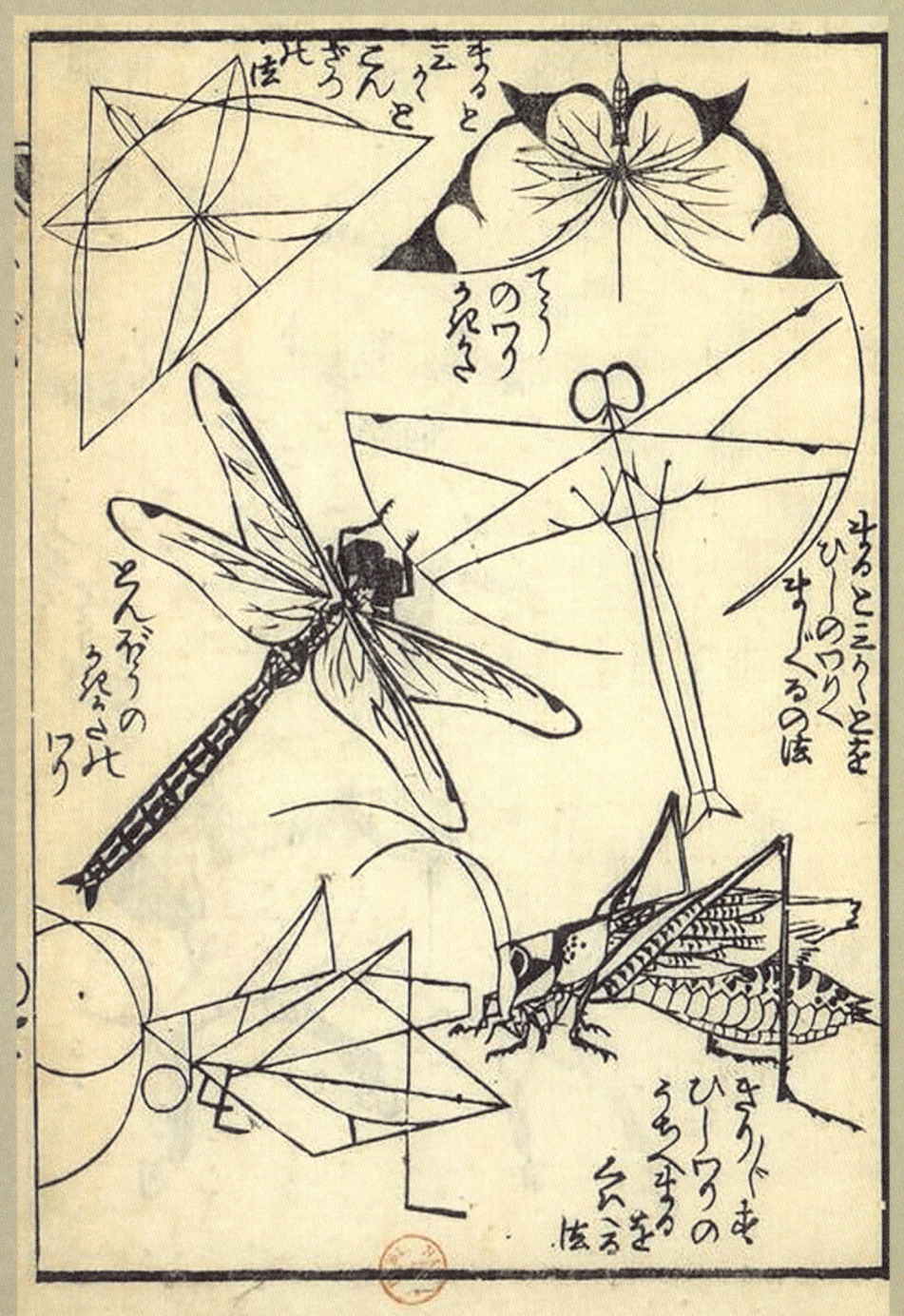

FIND SHAPES IN NATURAL FORMS

Let's see if we can find simple shapes—the circle, triangle, square, oval, and pentagon—in depictions of common natural subjects.

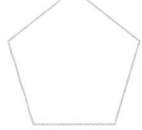

1. Many flowering fruit trees, leaves, and other natural forms have at their essence the pentagon or pentagram. Find the pentagon in this picture and lightly sketch it over the image.

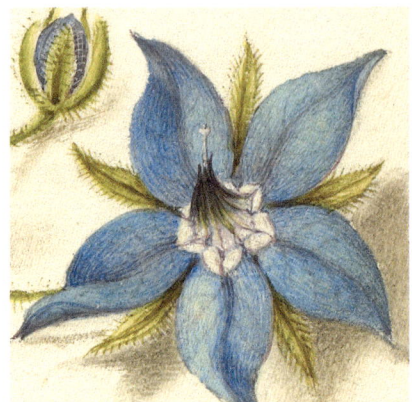

Joel Hoefnagel, *Detail of Speckled Wood, Talewort, Garden Pea, and Lantern Plant* (detail), 1561–62, watercolor, 6 ⁹⁄₁₆ x 4 ⅞ inches (16.6 x 12.4 cm), J. Paul Getty Museum

2. The square and other four-sided shapes can be found throughout nature in flowers such as the dogwood. Find the square and lightly sketch it over the image.

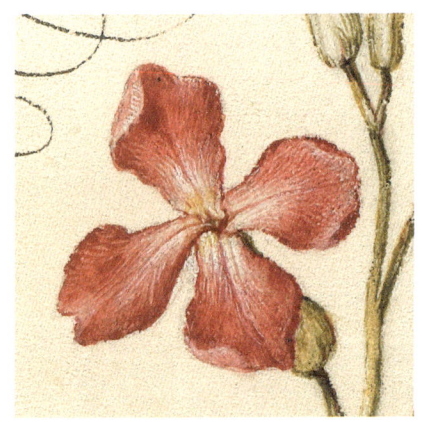

Joel Hoefnagel, *Reed Grass, French Rose, Toad, and Gillyflower* (detail), 1561–62, watercolor, 6 ⁹⁄₁₆ x 4 ⅞ inches (16.6 x 12.4 cm), J. Paul Getty Museum

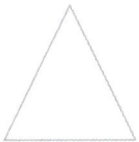

3. The triangle has strength and stability. You can see it in the pointy faces of cats as well as in fruit, birds, and planes. Find the triangle and lightly sketch it over the image.

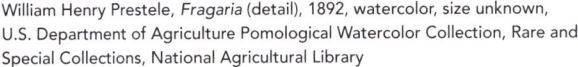

William Henry Prestele, *Fragaria* (detail), 1892, watercolor, size unknown, U.S. Department of Agriculture Pomological Watercolor Collection, Rare and Special Collections, National Agricultural Library

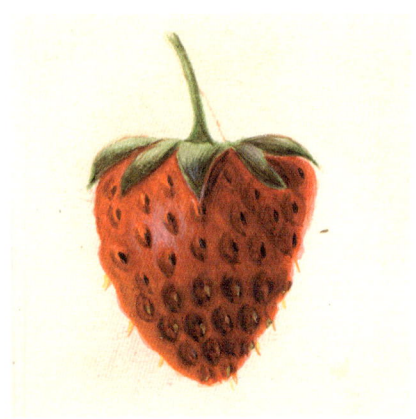

4. Find the hidden geometric framework in this drawing of insects and berries. Can you find the semicircle? Find as many triangles, circles, and ovals as you can and lightly sketch them over the image.

BELOW: Jan van Kessel II, *Butterfly, Caterpillar, Moth, Insects, and Currants*, ca. 1650–55, gouache and brown ink over underdrawing in metalpoint on vellum, 5 ⅛ x 6 ¹¹⁄₁₆ inches (13 x 17 cm), J. Paul Getty Museum

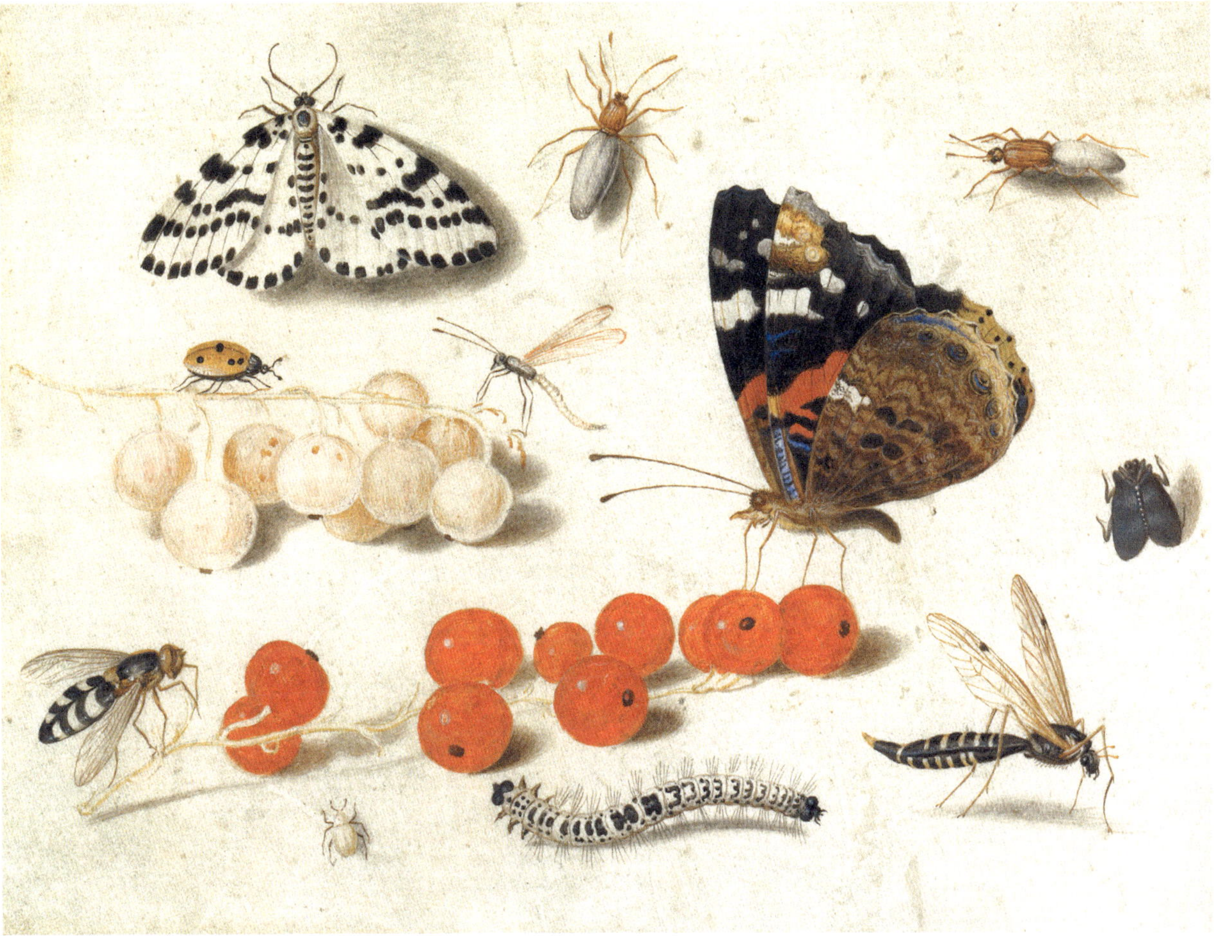

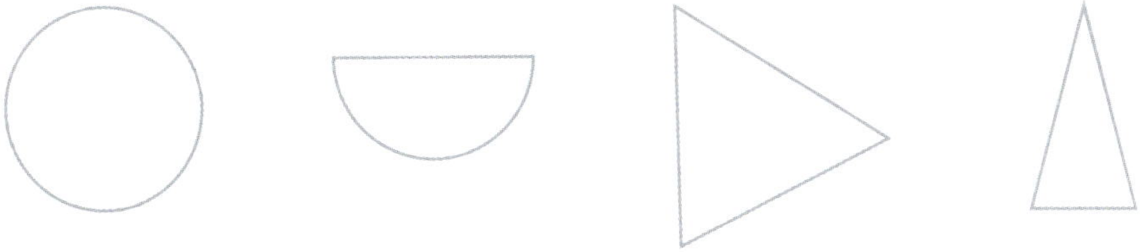

 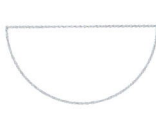 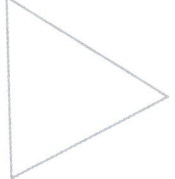 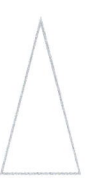

FIND A PENTAGRAM IN A LEAF

In this exercise, you will draw a star directly over the leaf opposite using the steps below. The goal here is to see and draw the essential pentagram (star) shape of a leaf, noticing that while all five-pointed (or pentagonal) leaves share the same underlying form, each is also unique. For this reason, some of our pentagons are fat, as on this page, while others are thin.

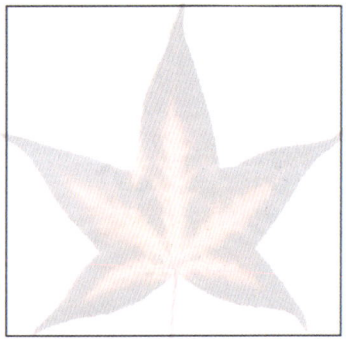

1. Very lightly draw a box snugly around the leaf.

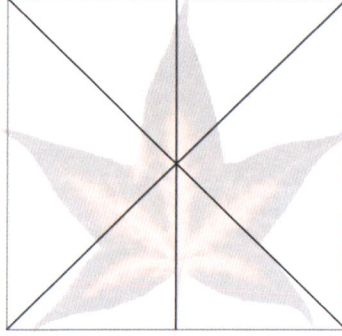

2. Find the center by **lightly** drawing an X from the corners and dropping a vertical through the middle point.

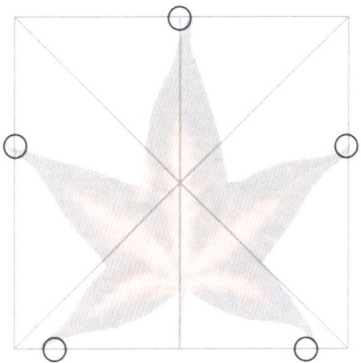

3. Mark where each leaf tip touches the box.

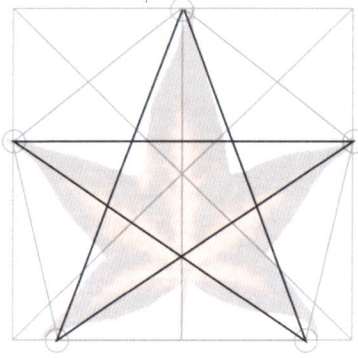

4. Connect all five points, making a pentagram.

*Each leaf, of oak and ash and thorn, is
a unique embodiment of the pattern,
and for some eye this very year may be
the embodiment, the first ever seen and
recognized, though oaks have put forth
leaves for countless generations of men.*

—J.R.R. TOLKIEN

DRAW FRUIT WITHIN A SHAPE

Let's explore the relationship between simple shapes and more subtle forms found in nature. For the images below and opposite, start by lightly drawing the outlining shape of a circle or triangle. Then sketch the leaf or fruit within it, taking care to notice how the natural object differs from the geometric shape.

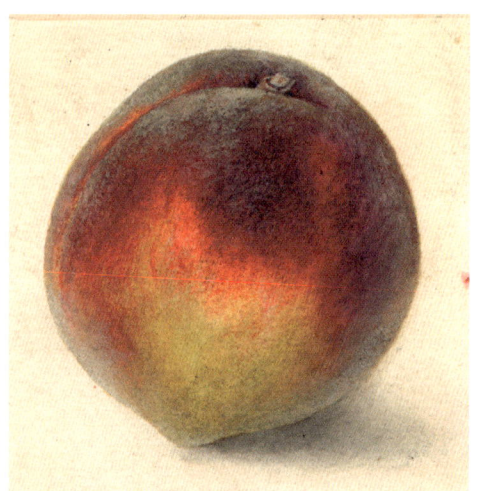

Deborah Griscom Passmore, *Prunus persica*, 1905, watercolor on paper, size unknown, U.S. Department of Agriculture Pomological Watercolor Collection, Rare and Special Collections, National Agricultural Library

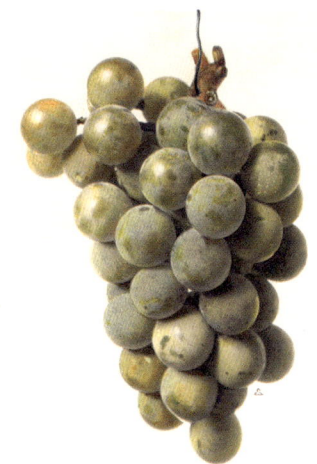

Royal Charles Steadman, *Vitis* (detail), 1934, watercolor on paper, 8 ⅜ x 10 ⅜ inches (22 x 27 cm), U.S. Department of Agriculture Pomological Watercolor Collection, Rare and Special Collections, National Agricultural Library

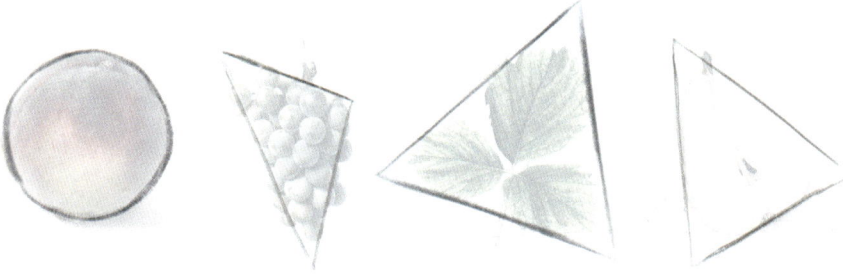

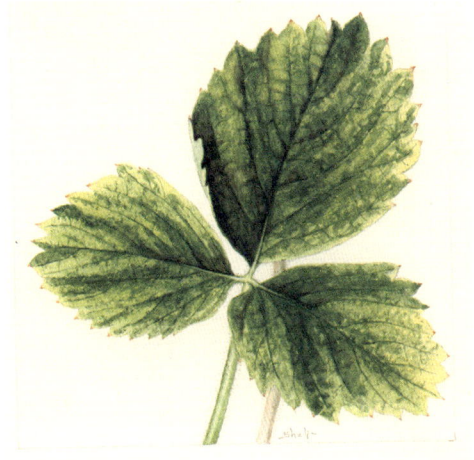

Ellen Isham Schutt, *Fragaria*, 1931, watercolor on paper, size unknown, U.S. Department of Agriculture Pomological Watercolor Collection, Rare and Special Collections, National Agricultural Library

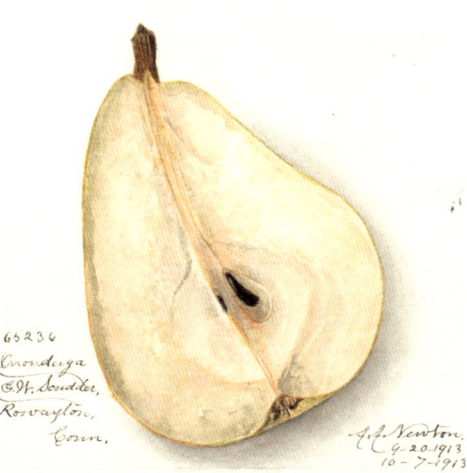

Amanda Almira Newton, *Pyrus communis*, 1913, watercolor on paper, size unknown, U.S. Department of Agriculture Pomological Watercolor Collection, Rare and Special Collections, National Agricultural Library

USE A UNIVERSAL SHAPE TO RE-CREATE A DRAWING

Find the dominant shape in this drawing of a cat and sketch it at the same size on the blank page opposite. Then use the shape as a guide to capture the cat's unique qualities.

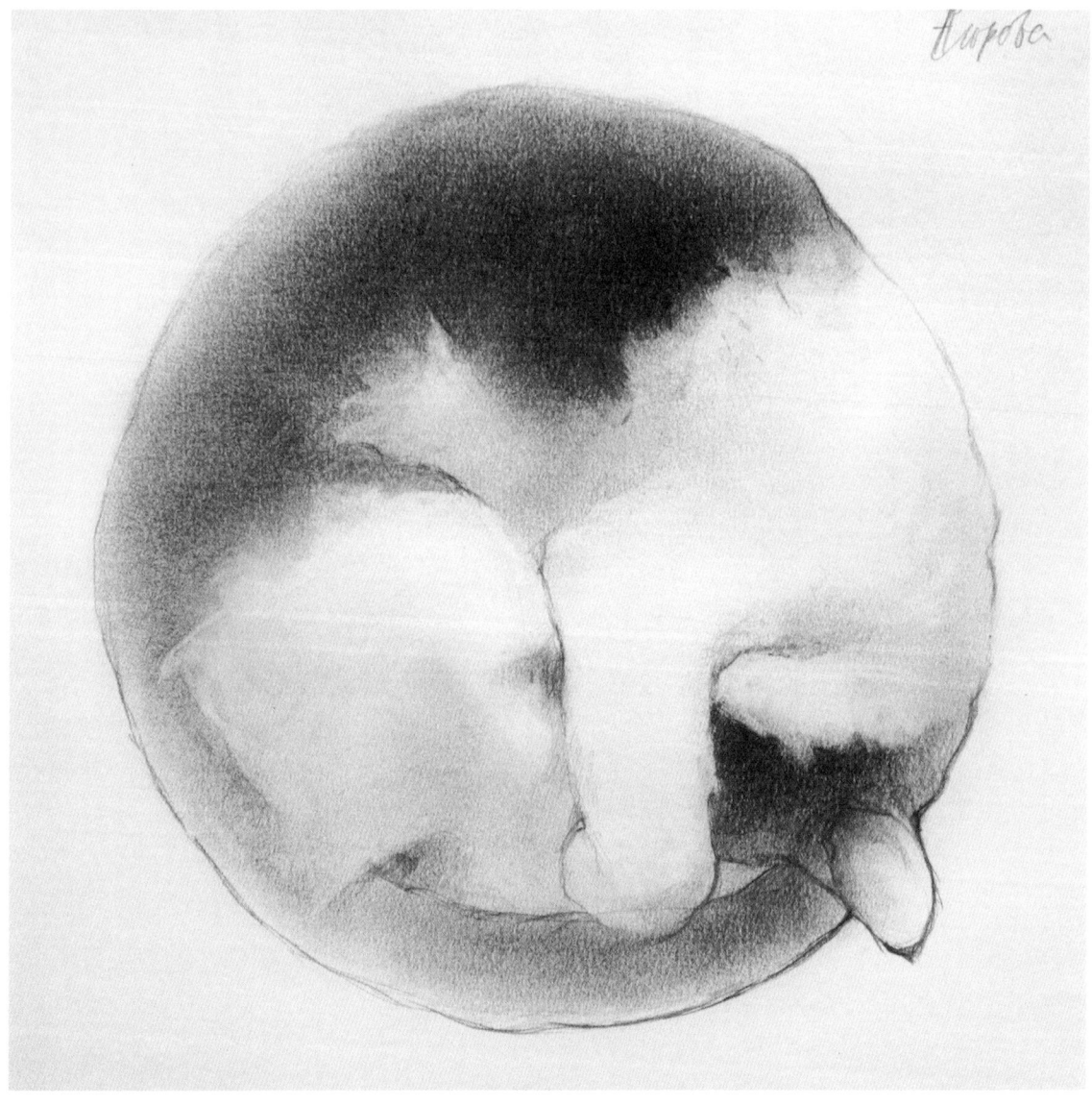

Anna Egrova, *Untitled*, 2013, graphite on paper, 7 ⅘ x 7 ⅘ inches (20 x 20 cm)

USE MULTIPLE SHAPES TO RE-CREATE A DRAWING

Instead of one circle delineating the whole shape of a cat, this drawing has a rhythm created by multiple circles. See if you can find the circles in the drawing and, through experimentation, re-create the picture on the page opposite.

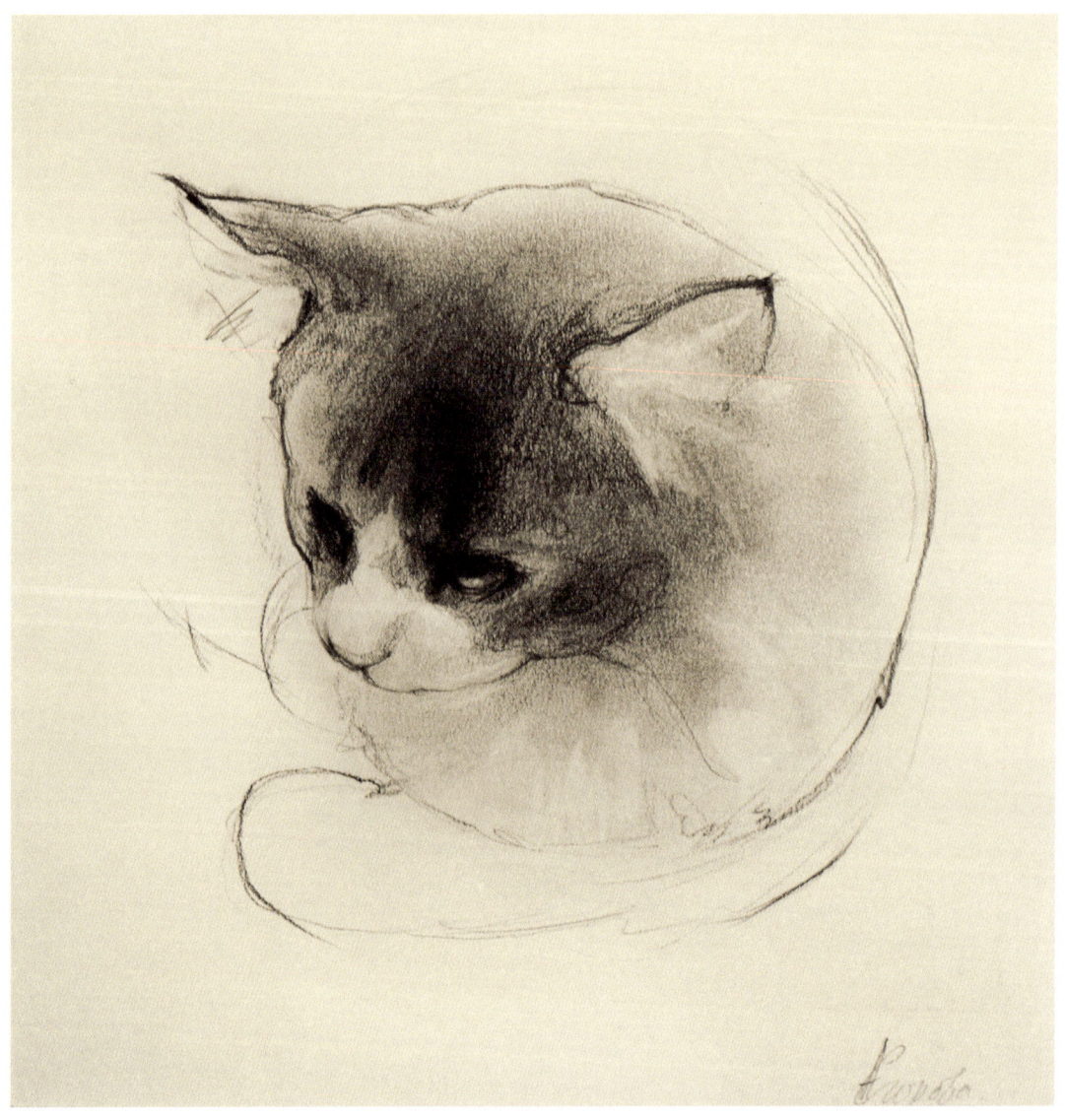

Anna Egrova, *Untitled*, 2013, graphite on paper, 7 ⅘ x 7 ⅘ inches (20 x 20 cm)

Blocking in your drawing

A block-in is created by distilling an object (or group of objects) into whatever shape speaks to you most clearly, such as a pentagram for the leaf on pages 38–39. Up to now we have focused on simple shapes, but drawing is rarely as direct as using a circle for a curled-up cat or a rectangle for a tissue box. Sometimes the shape is one we don't have a name for—like a triangle but squarer, or like a square but irregular. Happily, it's also true that few objects are as complex as they may appear. If I asked you to copy Leonardo da Vinci's sketch of a baby and lamb, shown opposite, you might at first find it intimidating. Yet if I asked you to first see and then replicate the triangle of the overall shape, it would be considerably easier. Try it.

To block in a mastercopy, start by laying down basic markers for the top and bottom of your drawing. Align a ruler (or the edge of a piece of paper) across the top of the master artwork and lightly mark the same point on your blank paper. Do the same for the bottom. Now you know how large your block-in should be.

Next, focus on the general outlined shape of your subject or composition and use a few straight lines—like pick-up sticks—to describe it. As an example, see the block-in I drew around Gerardus van Veen's *Standing Ruff,* on page 48. Think of this as scaffolding for the general shape of your subject. You can try this without drawing by taking toothpicks or wooden skewers (which can be cut down) and arranging them on images from books to create the best distillation of the subject.

To find the angles of your general shape, lay your pencil along the outline of your subject in the master artwork. Imagine your pencil is the short hand of a clock, pointing to an exact hour. Is it pointing to one o'clock? Eleven o'clock? Use this analogy to re-create the same angle on your blank paper. Continue to find the dominant angles until you've blocked in the shape of your subject. This first stage of a block-in is highly abstract; from it you would not be able to tell what your subject is, even if it is a person.

If you are drawing from life, use a variation on this technique. With your pencil (or a skewer or thin knitting needle) in your hand, hold your arm straight out like a police officer stopping traffic. Keep your elbow locked and the pencil parallel to your body. Hold the pencil so that when you close one eye (as you would to look through a telescope), the pencil appears to rest along the outline of your subject. Again, imagine that your pencil is the short hand of a clock, then match the angle of the pencil to the angle of your block-in to check for accuracy.

OPPOSITE: Leonardo da Vinci, *Studies for the Christ Child with a Lamb*, 1503–06, black chalk, pen, and brown ink on paper, 8 ¼ × 5 ⁹⁄₁₆ inches (21 × 14.1 cm), J. Paul Getty Museum

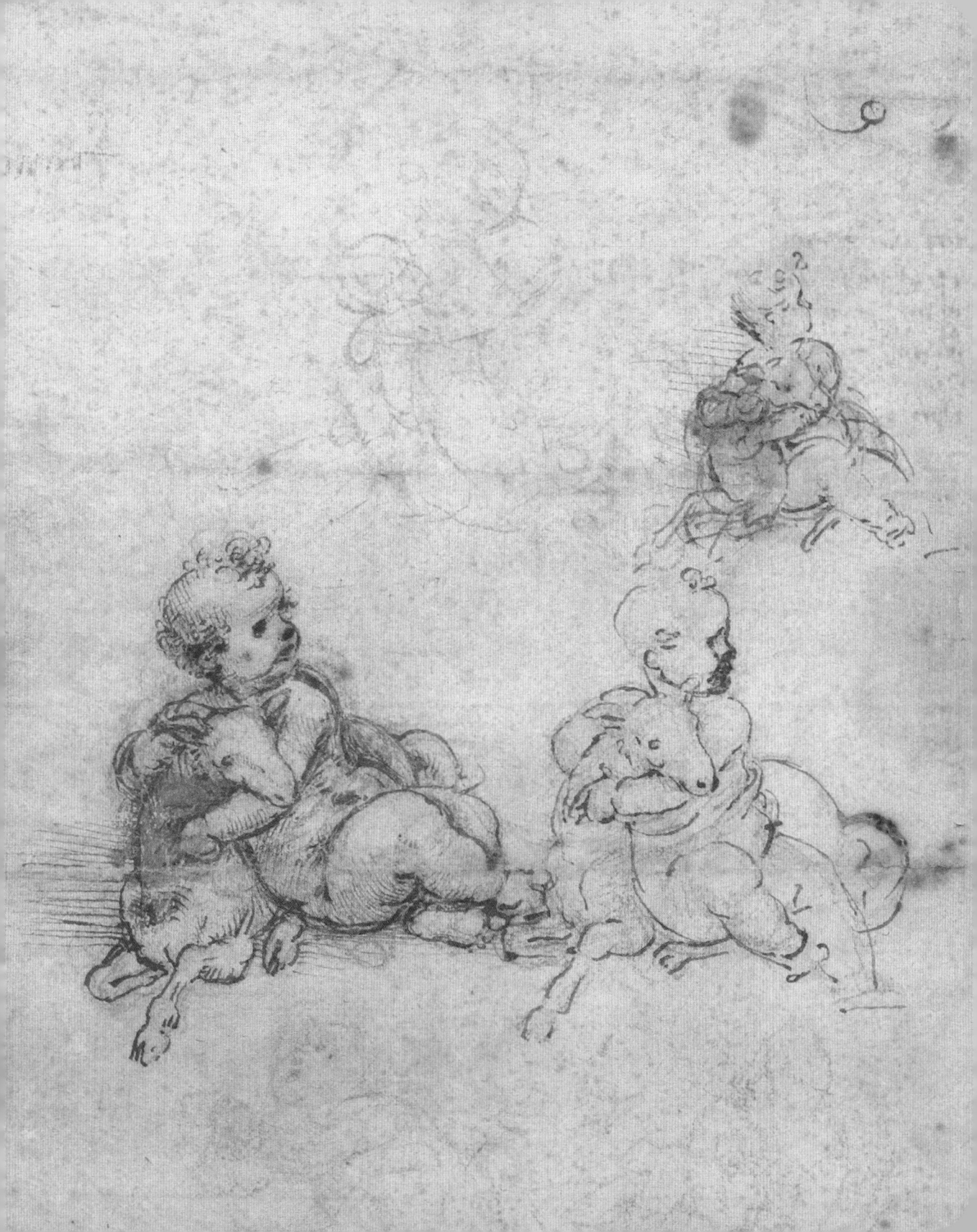

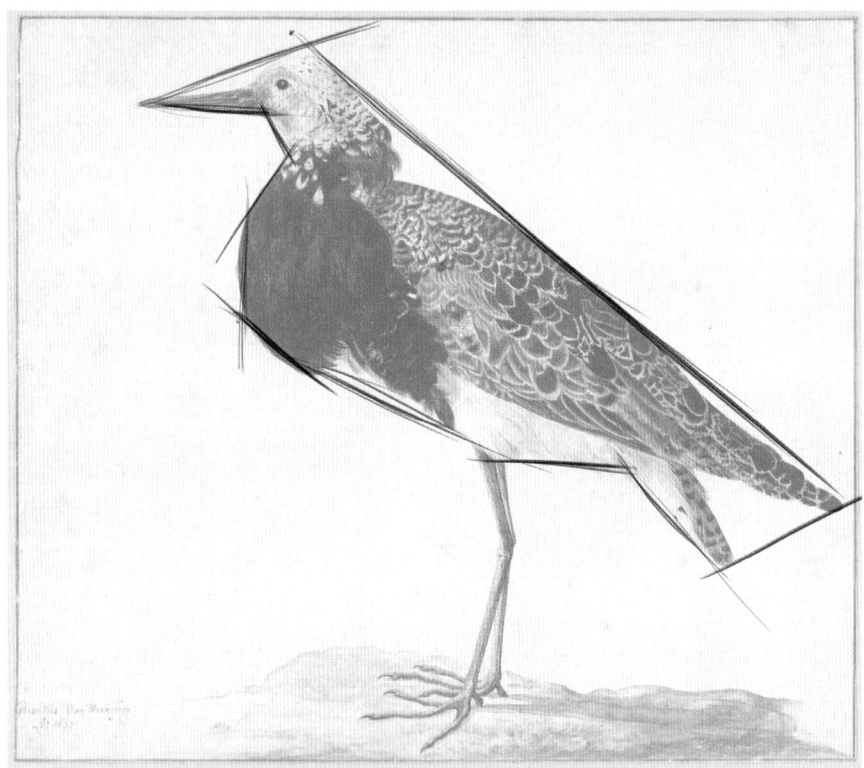

Start a block-in by drawing a general outlined shape around the subject.

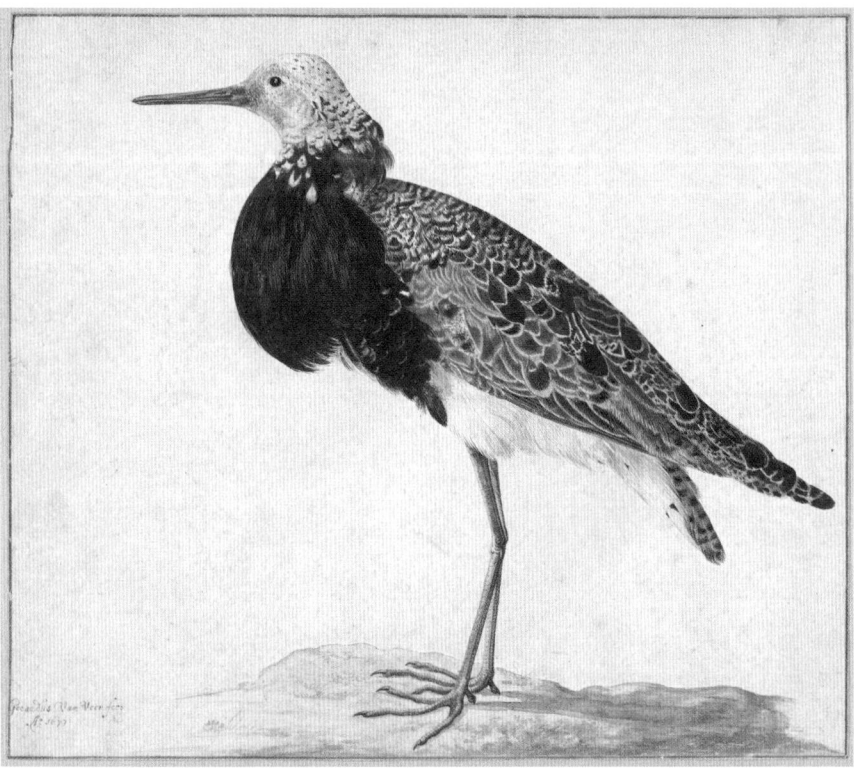

Gerardus van Veen, *Standing Ruff*, 1677, pen and brown ink, watercolor, and gouache over black chalk on paper, 9 3/16 × 10 11/16 inches (23.3 × 27.1 cm), J. Paul Getty Museum

BLOCK IN THE OUTLINED SHAPE

Use straight lines to block in a general shape around Théodore Géricault's *Seated Lion*, using the ghosted version below.

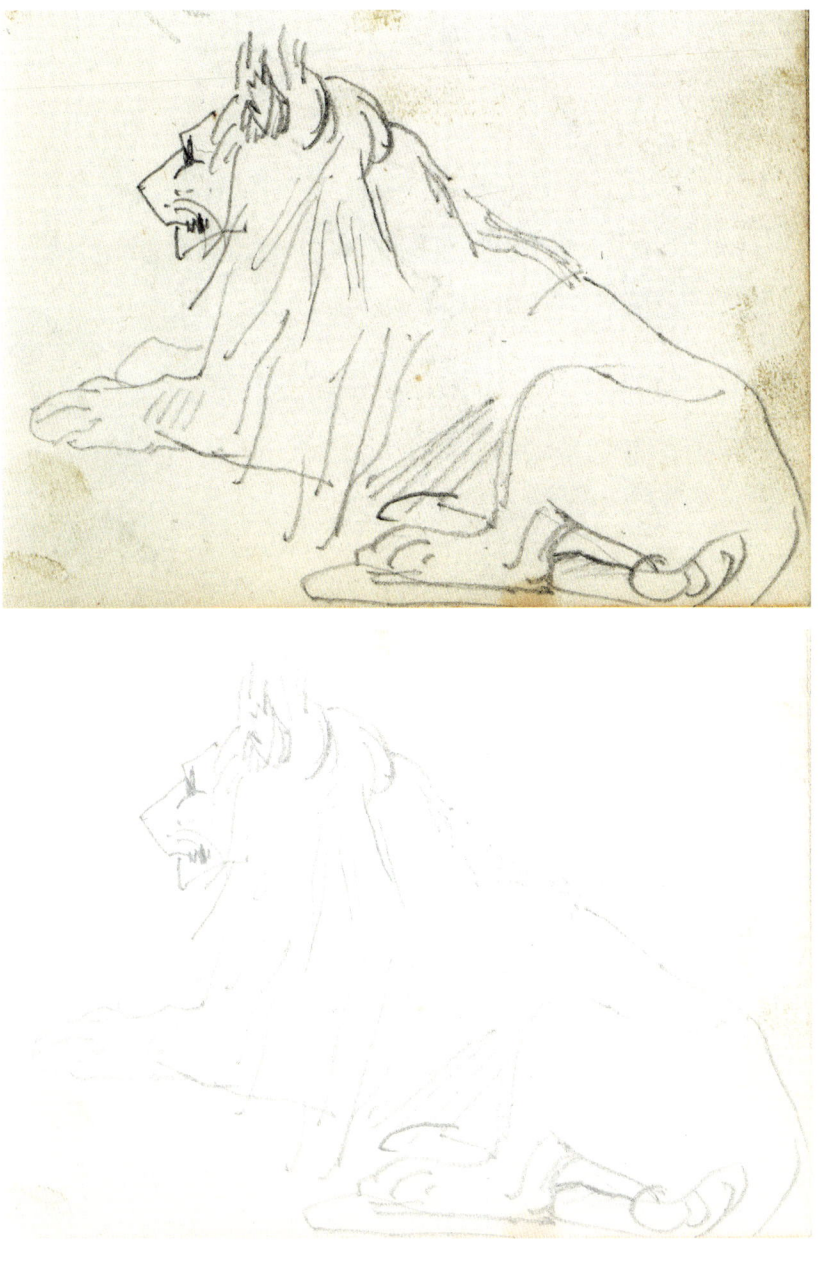

Théodore Géricault, *Seated Lion, two head studies* (detail), 1812–14, graphite on paper,
4 ³⁄₁₆ × 6 inches (10.6 × 15.2 cm), J. Paul Getty Museum

Refining your block-in

Once you've blocked in the outside shape or outline of your subject, the second stage is to refine your block-in by subdividing the large shape into smaller lines. Use the same technique described on page 46 to locate the shapes of shadows and smaller angles.

Once you have the largest elements of your drawing in place, take a few minutes to check it for accuracy using the tools on pages 58–63. Think of drawing as a dance between intuition and analytical thought: every so often you need to double-check your work. If things look reasonably placed, continue to find your secondary shapes.

We are always working from large to small forms. If your subject is a portrait, start by blocking in the shape of the head as a whole, check for accuracy, and then block in the secondary forms (in this case, the features).

Don't forget that shadow shapes are important parts of your subject matter and need to be blocked in now as well. By the end of your block-in stage, your subject should be fully mapped, including the shadows and contours.

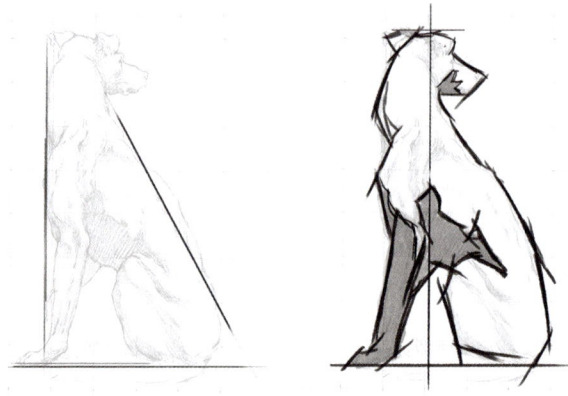

Start a mastercopy by blocking in the overall shape of your subject (top row, left), then refine the shape into smaller lines and angles (top row, right).

RIGHT: Kenyon Cox, *Hunting, Study for Panel*, ca. 1906, pencil on paper, 9 ¾ x 7 ⅝ inches (24.8 x 19.5 cm), Smithsonian American Art Museum (gift of Allyn Cox, 1959). Image courtesy of Art Renewal Center

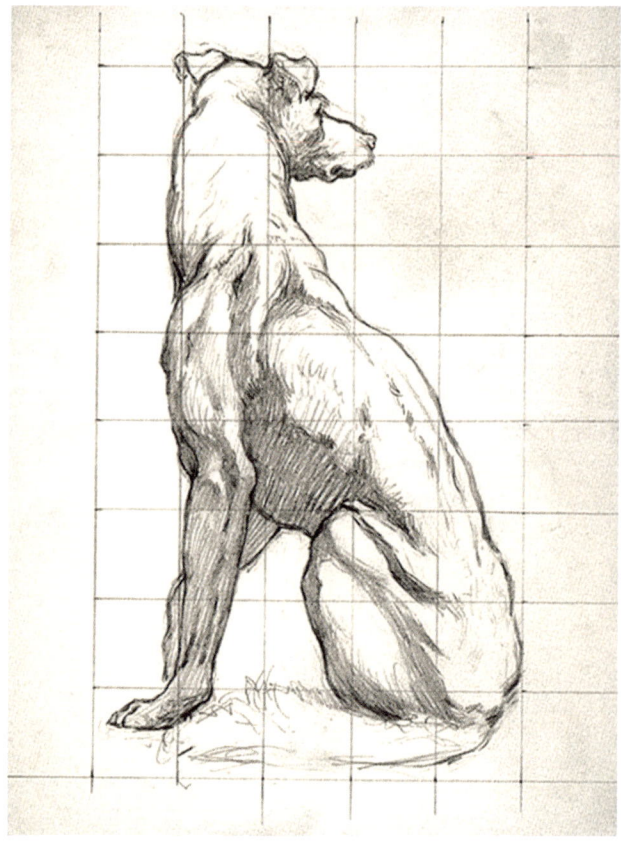

REFINE A BLOCK-IN

Over the ghosted version of Kenyon Cox's drawing of a dog, below, find a simple triangle shape, then break it down into a more detailed block-in.

BLOCK IN A STILL LIFE

Re-create the block-in of *Still Life with Lemon*, below, in the space opposite. When drawing a composition with multiple objects, start your block-in with an outlined shape of the overall still life. Then subdivide the outline into smaller lines to find the placement of individual objects, allowing those lines to become shapes. Finally, continue to refine the drawing, locating the shapes of the shadows and smaller angles. The small images opposite show examples of this progression.

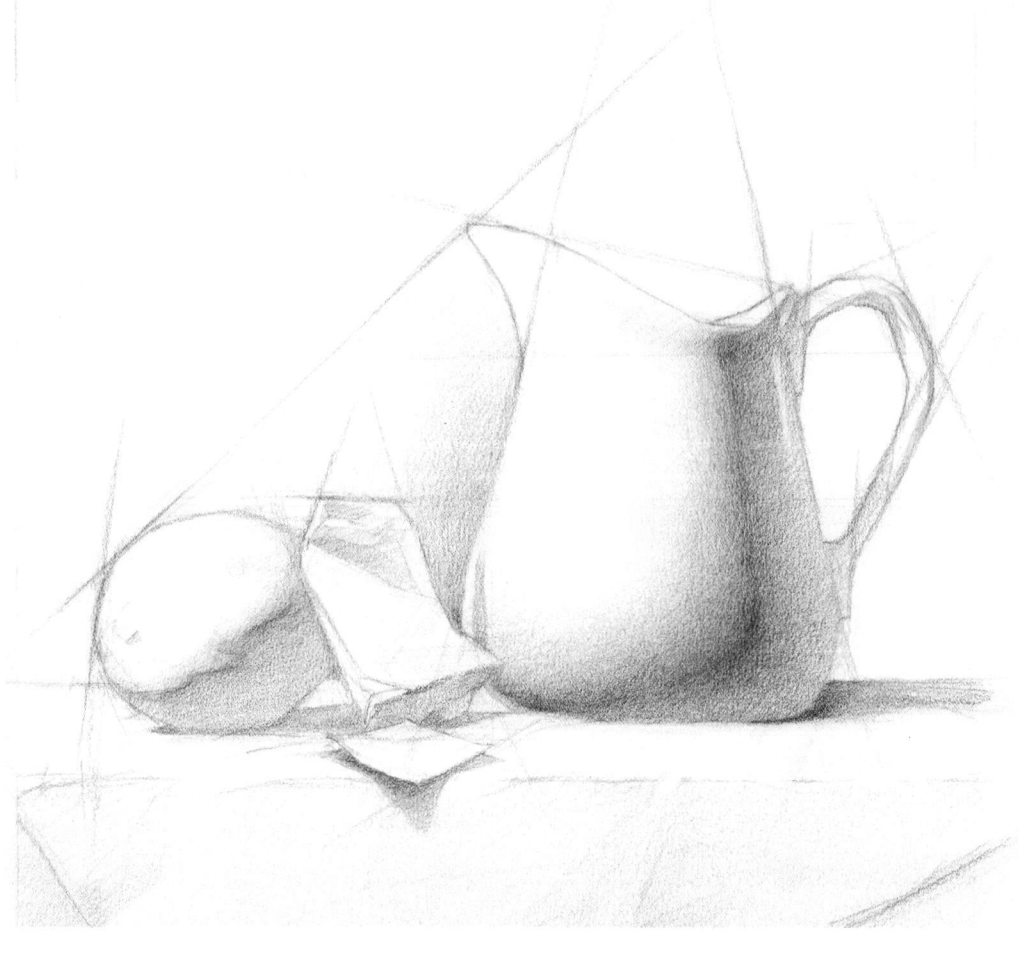

Ovidio Cartagena, *Still Life with Lemon* (detail), 2017, graphite on paper, 8 x 10 inches (20.3 x 25.4 cm), Aristides Atelier

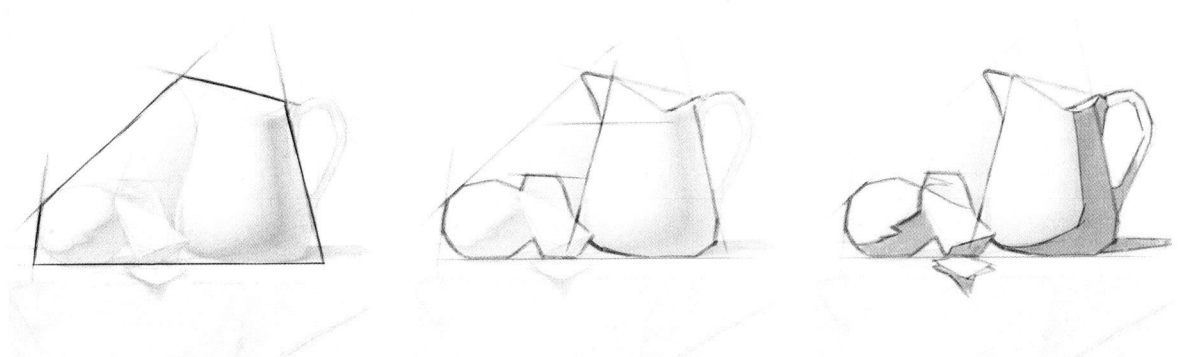

BLOCK IN IRREGULAR SHAPES

Block in this leaf and the cluster of apples on pages 56–57. As before, start by finding the angles of the outlined shape and then continue to refine the shape. My steps are shown as an example. Before you begin, lightly sketch the general shape on top of the finished drawing, below, to understand how they work together. Then sketch your drawing in the space provided, merging the three stages into one final drawing.

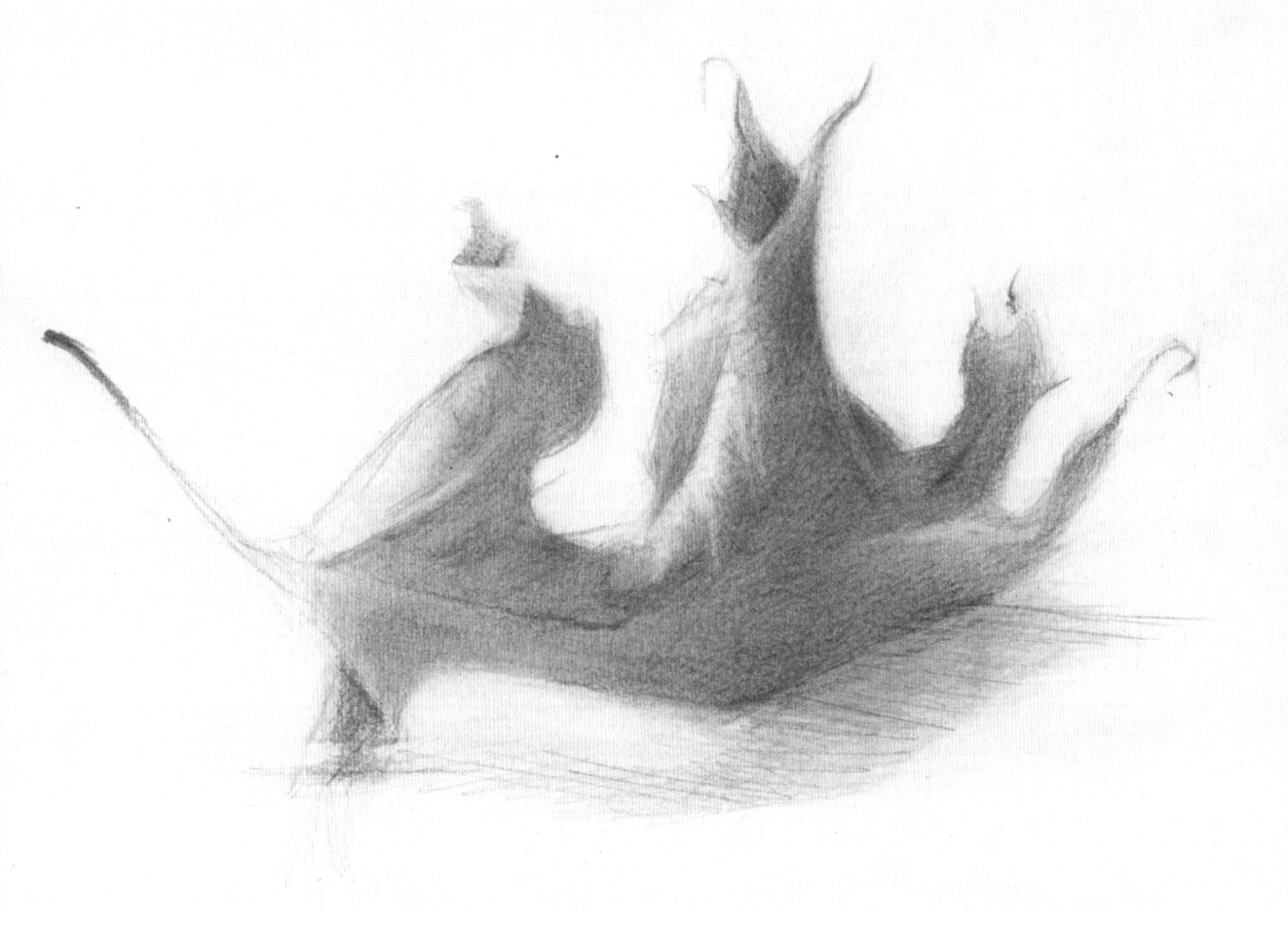

Juliette Aristides, *Leaf*, 2017, graphite on paper, 9 x 12 inches (22.9 x 30.5 cm)

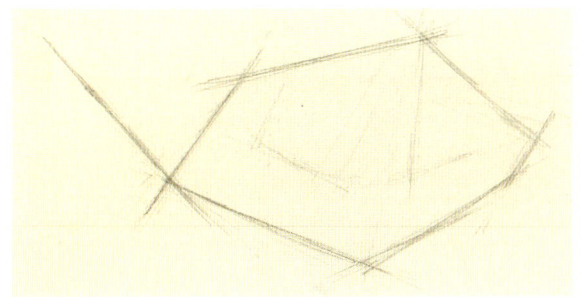 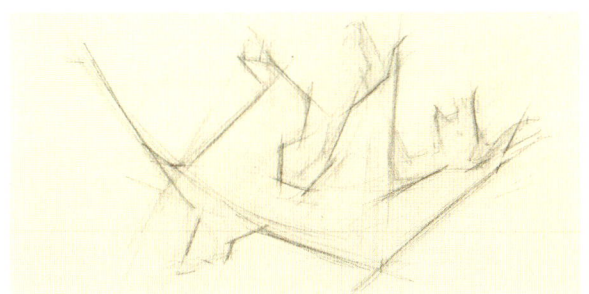

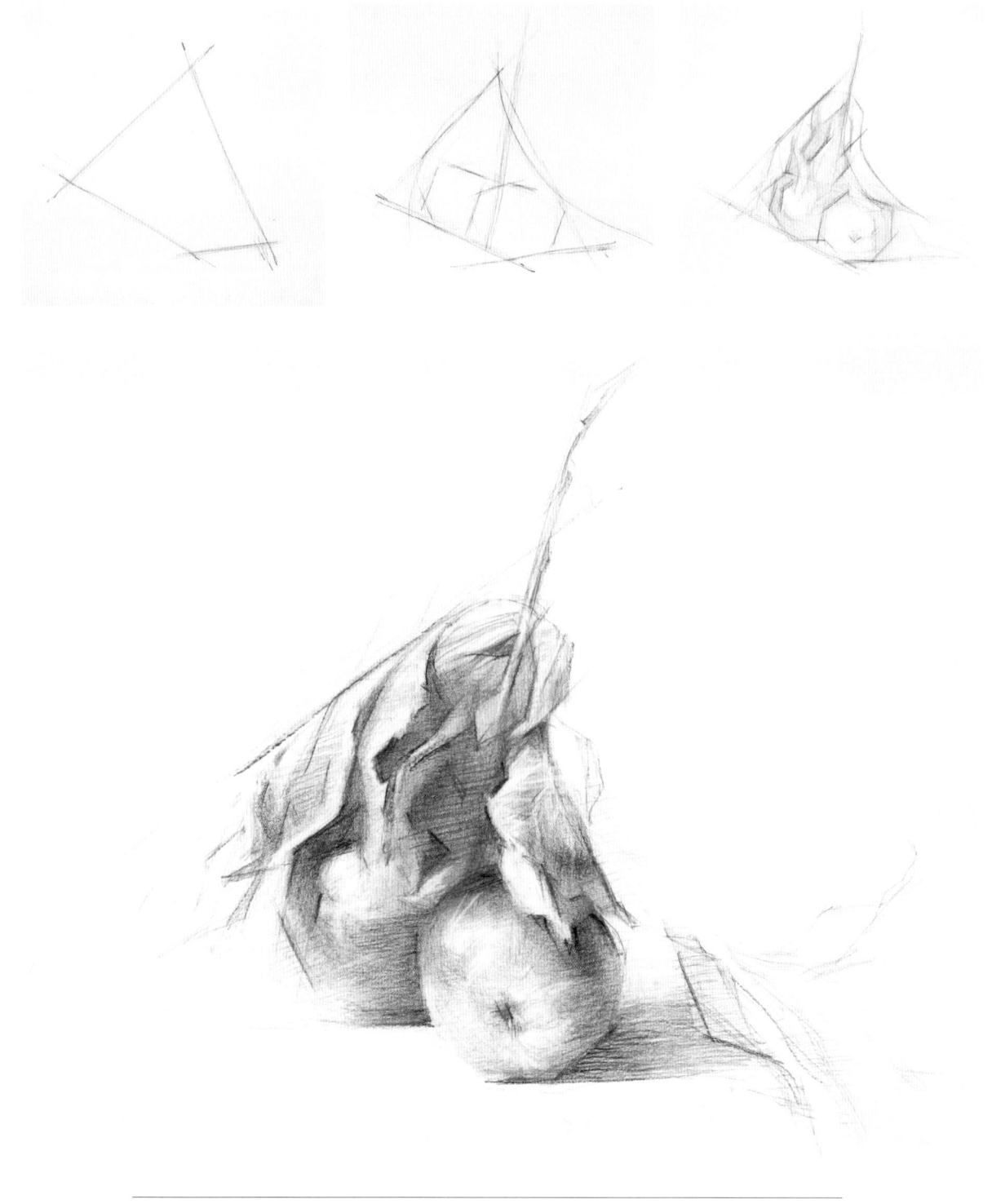

Juliette Aristides, *Apples*, 2017, graphite on paper, 9 x 12 inches (22.9 x 30.5 cm)

Checking for accuracy: Proportions

Until now, we have broadly placed the general shapes of our block-in relying predominantly on intuition and citing angles. But once your general block-in has been placed, it's time to check that it's as accurate as possible before continuing to refine it. One way to check for accuracy is to check proportions.

Proportion is the accurate relationship between parts and the whole. A simple way to check proportion is to compare the width-to-height ratio of your drawing with that of the master artwork (or real-life subject) to make sure they are the same.

Checking proportion is much easier to do if you don't look at the object itself, but assess it as a rectangle. When you are drawing, you may not choose to actually draw this rectangle on the page, and yet, when you assess width to height you are describing that shape. This imaginary rectangle that your object fits into is called *notional space*.

Start by inscribing a box around your object, like the square around the leaf on page 38. Use the widest and tallest points of your subject to determine the box's width and height, then connect these points to make a rectangle. Once you have the rectangle, measure the width and see how many times it fits into the box's height. Do the same with the master artwork (or your real-life subject). Are the proportions the same?

DEFINE A SUBJECT'S NOTIONAL SPACE

Draw directly over the images of the bugs on the opposite page to find their notional space, using my steps as examples. Here, I am using the bug at the top left as a demonstration. First, find the insect's center axis (A). Next, find the perpendicular line that best describes the top (B). This is not science but a judgment call. (In this example, I excluded the antennae because they did not feel significant, but you can decide for yourself what lines are useful.) This T-shaped configuration of the center axis perpendicular to the top is very useful when drawing, even if you take it no further. Then, brace the back end of the bug with a line parallel to the top (C). Lastly, frame the sides (D). This rectangle—the insect's notional space—will make it easier to assess its height and width.

A　　　　　　　B　　　　　　　C　　　　　　　D

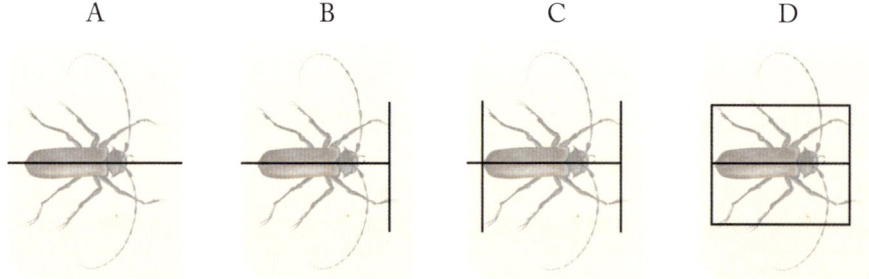

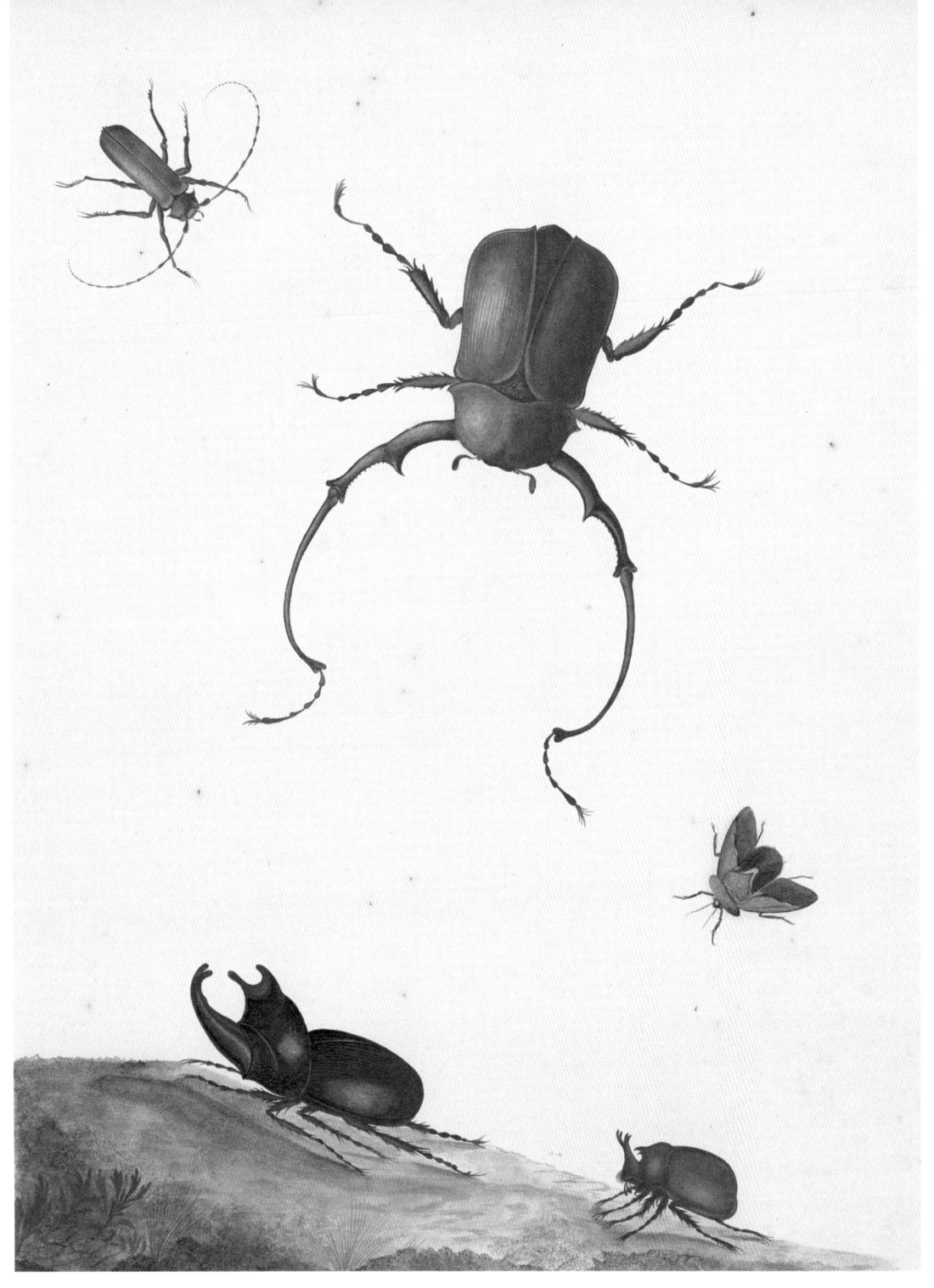

Nicolaas Stryck, *Four Beetles and a Flying Stink Bug*, 1715, pen and black ink, watercolor, gouache, gold paint with white gouache heightening, and pen and brown iron-gall ink on paper, 17 ³⁄₁₆ x 11 ¼ inches (43.7 x 28.6 cm), J. Paul Getty Museum

Checking for accuracy: Measuring

A second tool for checking your block-in's accuracy is measuring. Measuring for accuracy is all about finding a reliable unit and then using it consistently as a ruler to double-check your intuition. As G. K. Chesterton wrote, "A man might measure heaven and earth with a reed, but not with a growing reed."

Choose something in your block-in that feels stable and significant—perhaps a head length or the width of an apple—and use it as a unit of measure. As long as you are consistent, the drawing will turn out correctly. If you are sketching a still life, choose how many times one element of it, such as a cup, goes into the whole. At a minimum, find the halfway point on your subject and check the overall width to height so that the most basic proportions are correct. If something feels off in the drawing later, you will know it's not these foundational points.

Measuring techniques differ if you are drawing a mastercopy versus drawing from life. To check a mastercopy, use a ruler, triangle, or even just a blank piece of paper to draw a straight line from the top of the master drawing across to the blank page, then repeat across the bottom. To measure the halfway point of the subject, lay your pencil or a scrap of paper against the drawing to find the midpoint, then compare it to your drawing. Are they the same? To find the widths, use the same straightedge as before and mark off the width to check against your copy. Later in the drawing, you can check the alignment of smaller measurements against your work. Give it your best guess first and check later; that way, you can continue to refine your eye.

If you are drawing from life, use your pencil (or a skewer) and hold it as you did to find the block-in angles, keeping your arm straight and the pencil perpendicular to your arm. Keep the tip of the pencil touching the top of your unit of measure and slide your thumb until it hits the bottom. If you are using the head length of a standing figure, the top of the pencil should touch the top of the head and your thumb should lock in the chin. Now keep that unit fixed and your arm straight as you use the pencil and your "head" unit of measure to check other parts of the drawing. For example, if there are three "head" units between your live subject's chin and his belt buckle, make sure your drawing reflects the same.

OPPOSITE: Honoré (firm), porcelain sample catalog (with overlay), ca. 1800–20, watercolor, gouache, ink, and graphite on paper, 9 ¼ x 6 ½ inches (23.5 x 16.5 cm), J. Paul Getty Museum

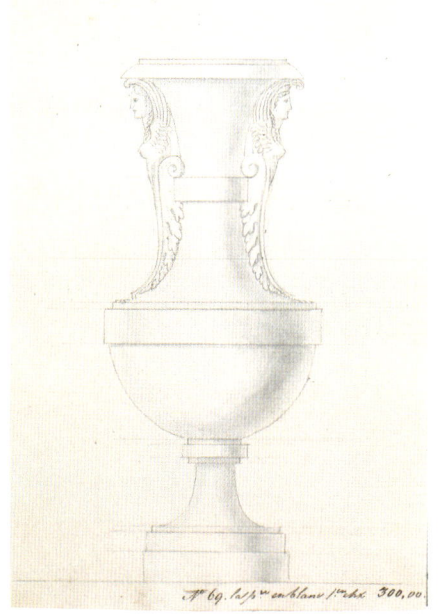

1. Can you find the notional space around this vase?

2. Use the width to make a square (labeled "1").

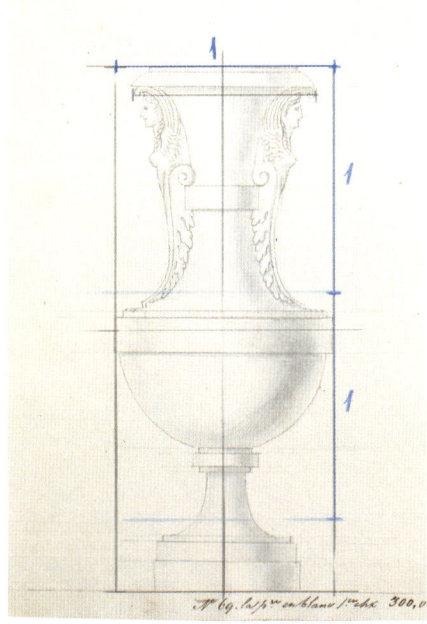

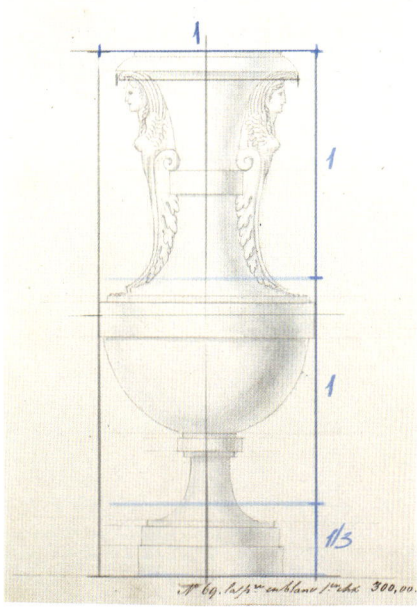

3. Use the same unit of measure to mark another square.

4. This vase is 2 ⅓ squares high.

CHECK A SUBJECT'S PROPORTIONS

Let's go a step further, using notional space and measuring to check proportions. Use the steps on page 58 to draw a rectangle around the silhouette in the ghosted version below. Next, measure the width of the figure. You don't need a ruler; just place your pencil against the drawing and use that as your unit of measure. How many times does the width go into the height? On the opposite page, re-create the silhouetted figure by drawing the imagined box or notional space in the blank area provided before sketching the figure. Check how many head lengths measure into the whole.

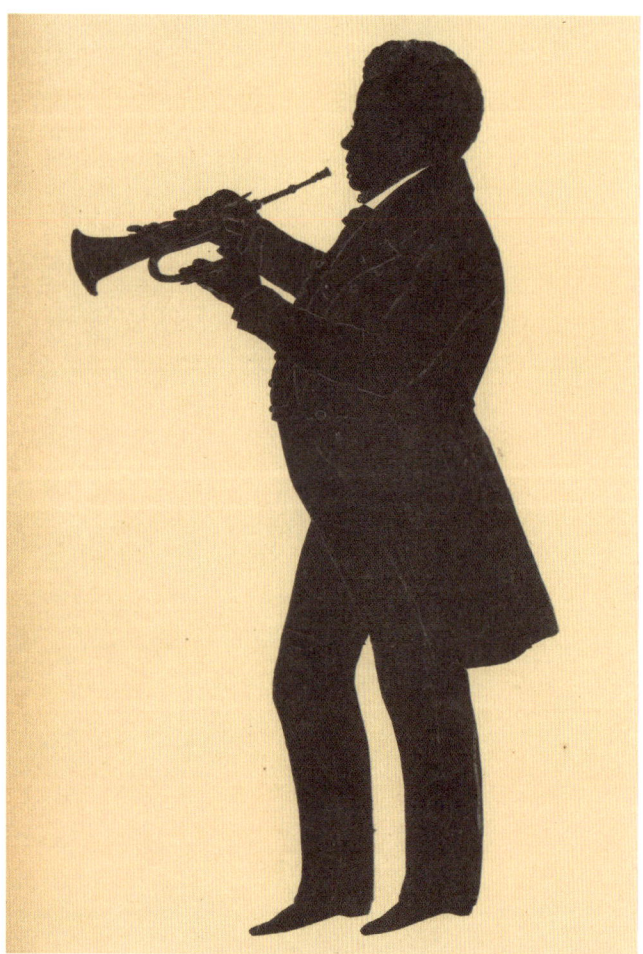
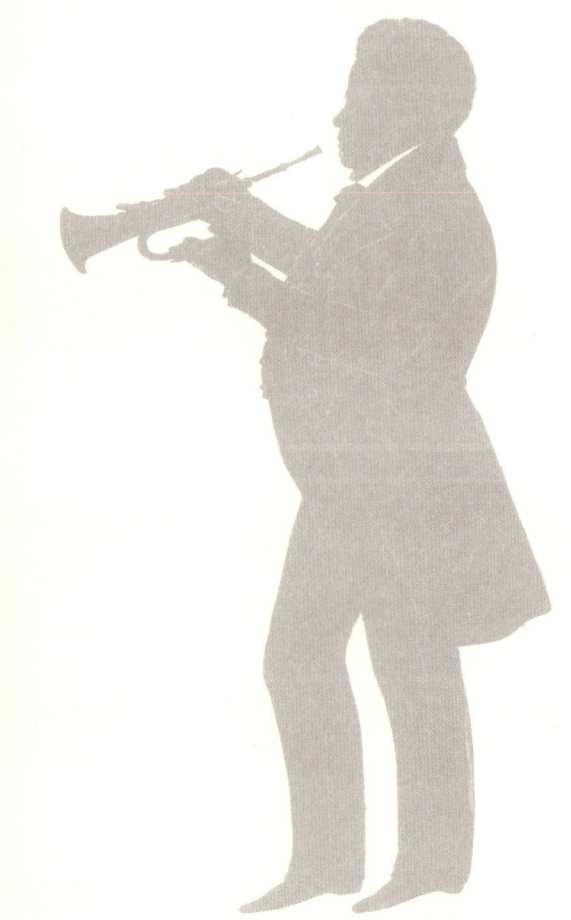

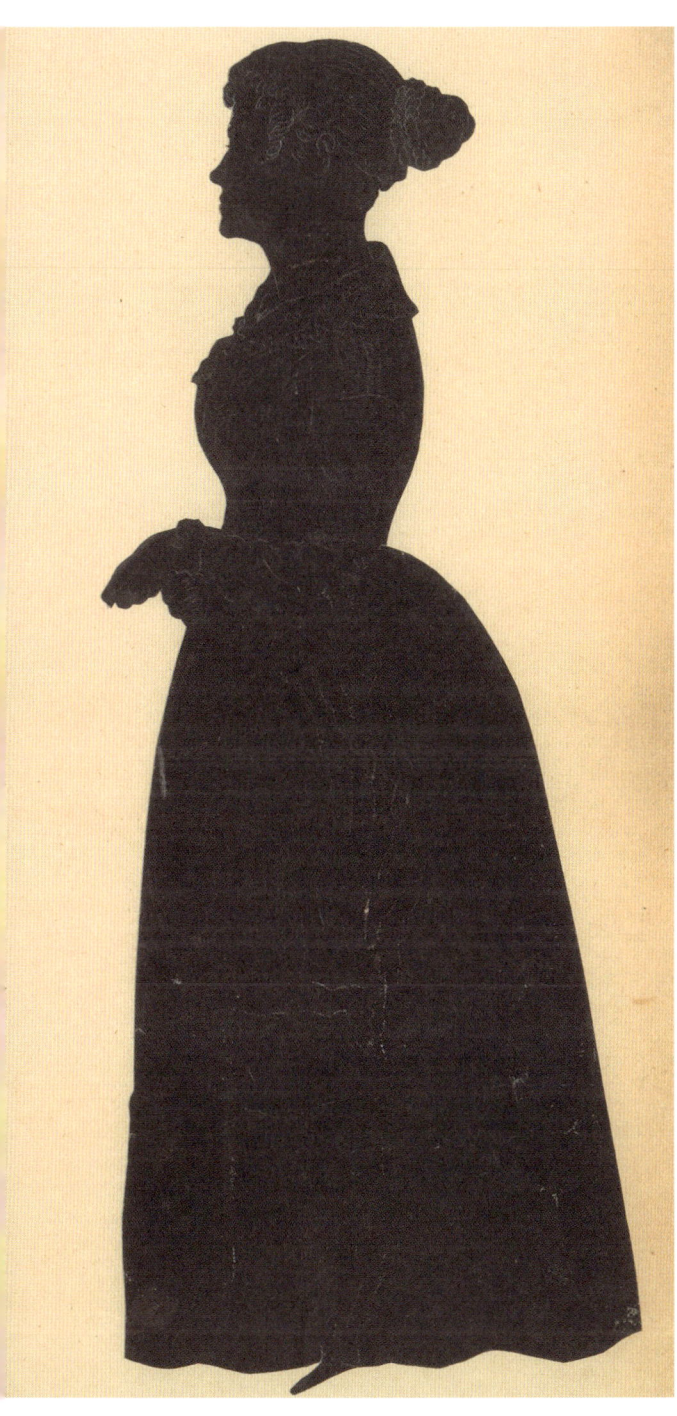

OPPOSITE AND ABOVE: Auguste Edouart, *Frank Johnson, Leader of the Brass Band of the 128th Regiment in Saratoga, with His Wife, Helen* (detail), ca. 1842–44, cut paper silhouettes mounted on board, 11 5/16 x 9 5/16 inches (28.8 x 23.6 cm), Metropolitan Museum of Art (gift of Philip S. P. and Elisabeth W. Fell, 1976)

MEASURE FOR ACCURACY

Draw this pineapple by marking the top, bottom, and halfway of the illustration on the blank page opposite. Next, find the vertical centerline. Now lightly block in the shapes of your pineapple freehand. When you are finished, measure the width and height of your drawing and compare it with the master artwork.

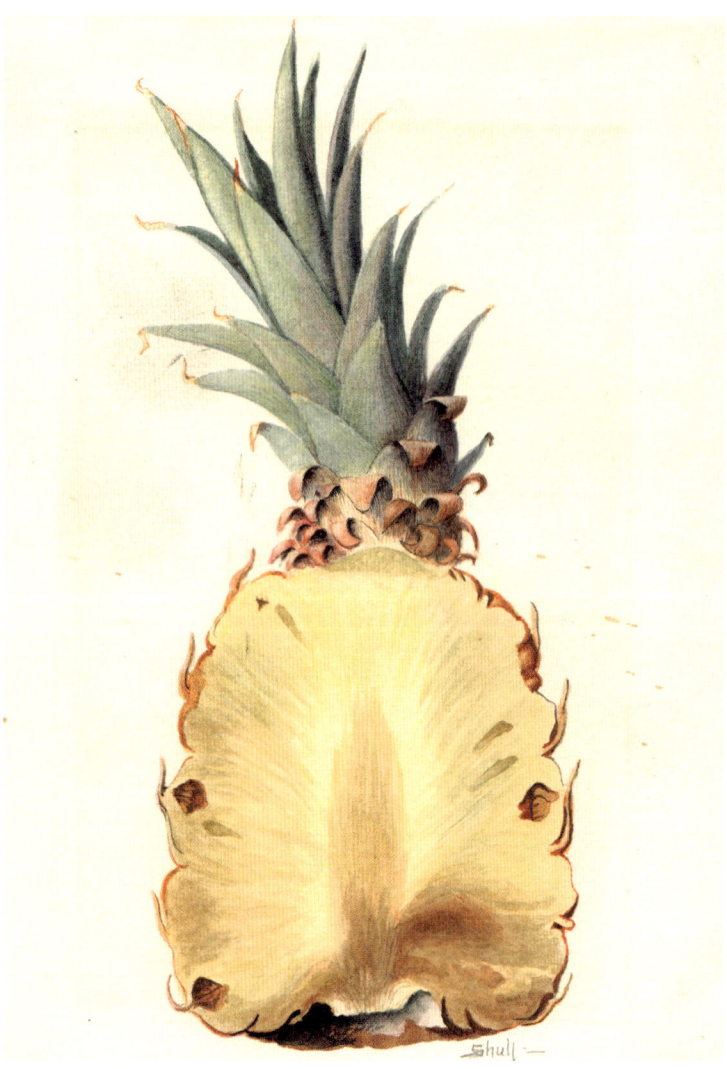

James Marion Shull, *Ananas comosus [Pineapple]*, 1919, watercolor on paper, U.S. Department of Agriculture Pomological Watercolor Collection, Rare and Special Collections, National Agricultural Library

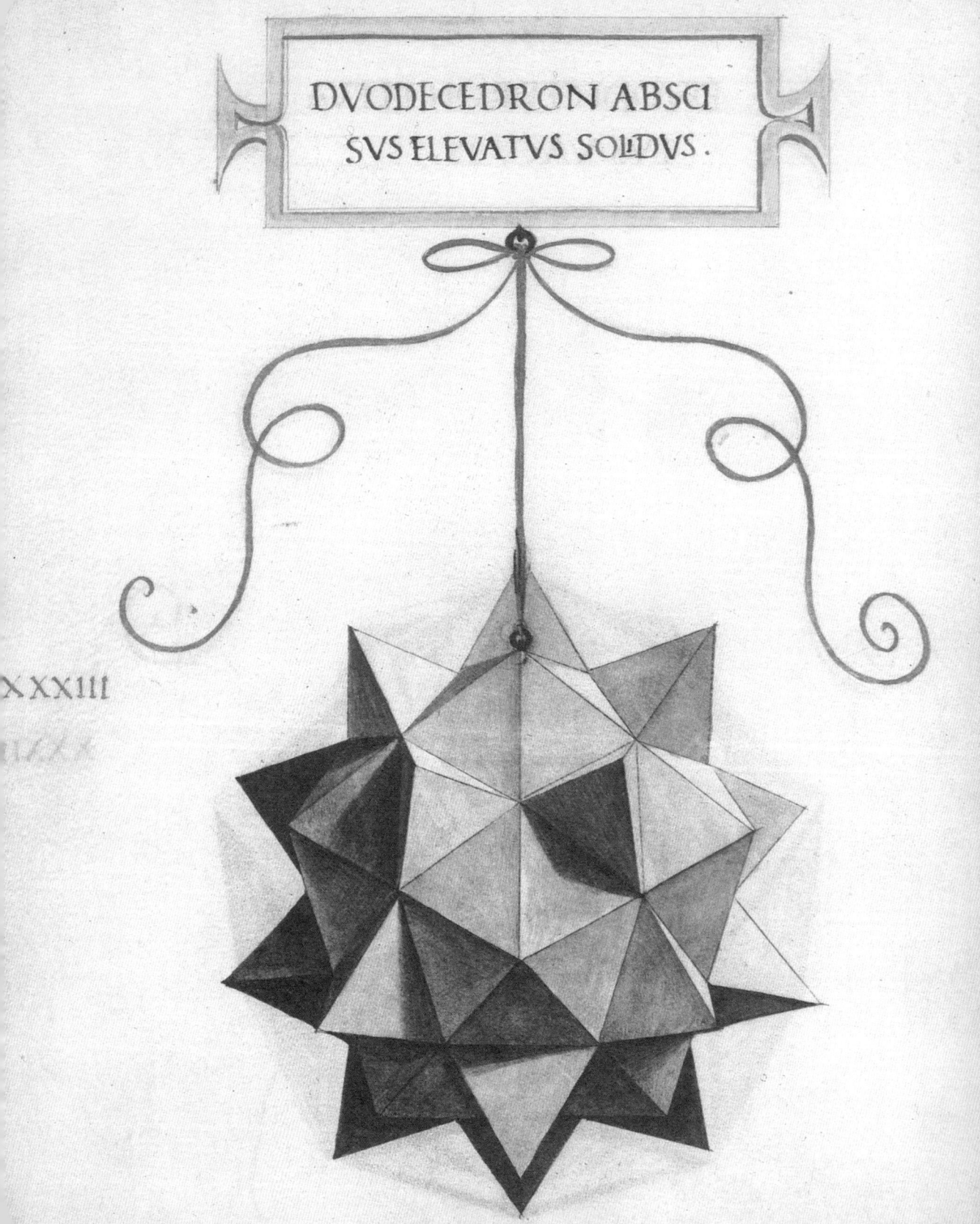

XXXIII

THREE

VOLUME

*May I repeat what I told you here: treat nature by means of the cylinder,
the sphere, the cone …*

—PAUL CÉZANNE, LETTER TO ÉMILE BERNARD, 1904

This book follows the creation of a drawing. In the beginning is a *point*, indicating a location with no mass. When we place a second point, we create a *line* showing direction: a vector. Once the angle is correctly located, we add more lines to block in a *shape*. This shape, or surface, covers a specific area—it has scale and proportion, and maybe even character in the contour—but it flattens our object, reducing it to two dimensions. To create weight and have things sit properly in space, without ambiguity, we must show more than one plane, preferably three: height, depth, and width. So we move into *volume*. With each of these steps—from point to line, shape, and volume—the drawing gains solidity and weight.

Think of this chapter as a sidebar, or a pullout section for additional study. You can do beautiful drawings without understanding how volumes sit in space; however, it will help you better envision the shapes of your forms when sculpting them with tone (discussed in chapter 5). Understanding volume will help you wrap your mind around what you are seeing, to more easily conceive of complex objects as a series of shapes. Don't think of this section as its own stage, but rather as a way of informing your drawing with subtle clarity. Also, since we encounter ellipses often in drawing, the exercise on pages 68–69 will give a feel for how they are supposed to look so that you can draw them freehand with more accuracy.

OPPOSITE: Leonardo da Vinci, *Duodecedron Absci Sus Elevatus Solidus*, 1509, illustration for *De Divina Proportione* by Luca Pacioli. Image courtesy of Art Renewal Center

The building blocks of volume

While writing this, I am sitting at my kitchen table, looking around the room to find examples of geometric solids. I gradually notice that everything in my line of sight was created with simple shapes, like children's building blocks. The electric kettle is conical, the fridge a block, the paper towels a cylinder, the teacup a half-sphere. Looking out the kitchen window to the trees and bushes is another story; they form wild shapes that defy quick analysis. Upon deeper inspection, however, the same principle applies. I start to see the cypress tree as a cylinder and the magnolia as a sphere.

To create depth in any subject, it helps to envision it as simple solids. Using these solids as a starting point, we then combine them to create more complex forms. Even the most complex objects can be seen as combinations of simple geometric solids. This is also true for things of vastly differing sizes. Using our imagination, we can see the same shape in a skyscraper as in a bar of soap. The bulging ball in the dome of a cathedral echoes the sphere in the belly of my teapot. In our man-made designs, straight lines and formalized shapes make objects easier to manufacture.

DRAW AN ELLIPSE

To draw a cone, sphere, or cylinder, it's helpful to be able to first draw an ellipse. I often study the ellipses made by liquid in a glass, tilting the glass to see the ellipse change direction. Even easier, hold a coin so it's perfectly round, then start tipping it away from you and watch the circle become oblong.

In the demonstration opposite, the three images across the top show how to draw a basic ellipse. Start with a square or rectangle and then find the diagonals to form an X. Next, add the center vertical and horizontal lines to form a cross (A). Connect the midpoints of each side to form a center diamond shape, then tick a mark on each diagonal halfway between the sides of the diamond and the corner of the square (B). This configuration locates the points you need for a basic circle (C).

The second row shows you how an ellipse looks on planes in perspective. The number-one mistake for beginners is to draw the curve of the ellipse almond-shaped and pointy, rather than rounded, as it touches the edges of the rectangle.

Fill in the last four rectangles with the missing information to generate an ellipse. I started two of them for you.

A B C

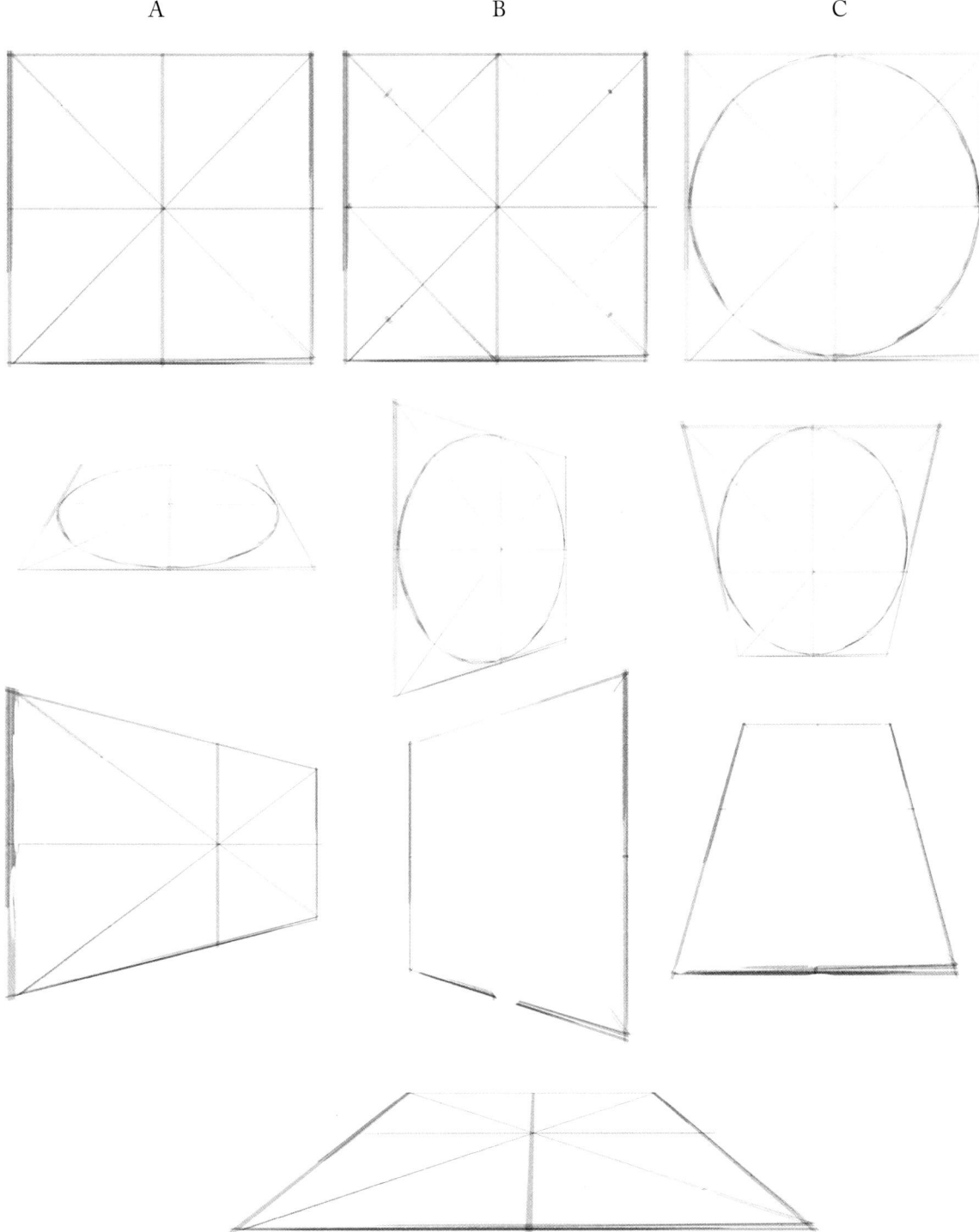

DRAW GEOMETRIC SOLIDS

Practice drawing simple geometric solids—cubes, spheres, cylinders, cones, and pyramids—freehand until they become familiar, so that they spring to mind at will. Later, you can apply them to subjects of increasing complexity to infuse your work with greater understanding. Note that this is only a cursory exposure to these volumes. We are not introducing perspective here as it is beyond the scope of this book.

To make a cube, start with a square and then find two other planes. Be sure to use only *three* line directions: vertical, horizontal, and *one* additional line. Using many different angle directions will derail your drawing.

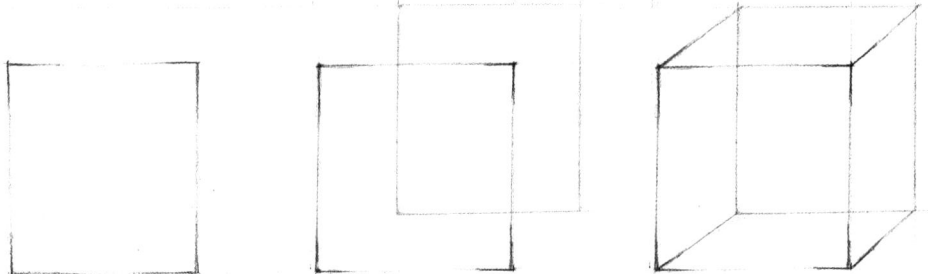

The cone is the simplest form: start with a triangle and then add an ellipse at the bottom. Make sure the edges of your ellipse stay curved as they wrap around the base of the cone, shaped like the top of an egg, not pinched like the pointy end of a teardrop.

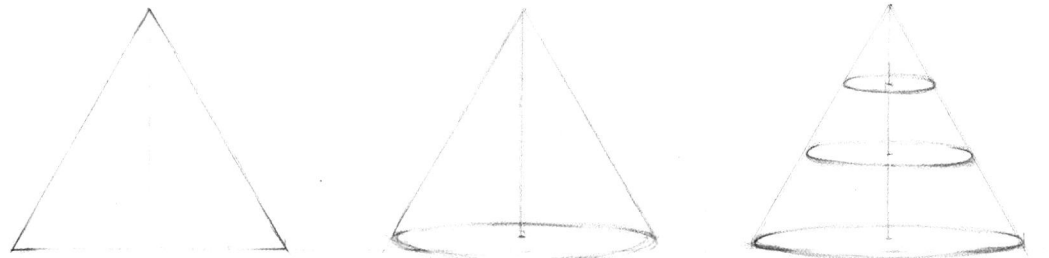

To make a sphere, envision a ball. Start with a circle and then add a straight line as the central axis, like a spoke going through a globe. Take a coin and hold it between your fingers. Slowly turn it, noticing all the ellipses created without it actually changing the shape of the outside circle. Even easier, spin your coin on the table like a top and watch how it appears to be a full sphere rather than a flat plane. When drawing a sphere, you do not need to create all the ellipses; two are enough to get the idea.

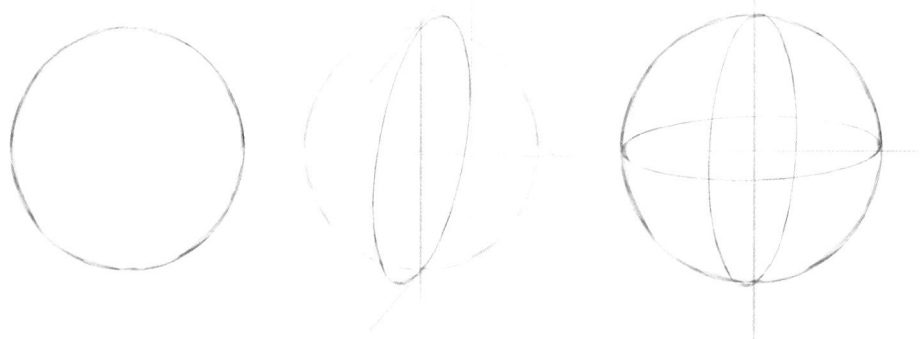

If you look at a cylinder at eye level, it is just a rectangle. When viewed from an angle, however, its rod-shaped volume becomes apparent. This is conveyed in your line drawing by adding ellipses at the top and bottom. In this exercise, use the two short ends of the rectangle as the center horizontal axis to plot your two ellipses. You can freehand the ellipses or follow the steps on pages 68–69.

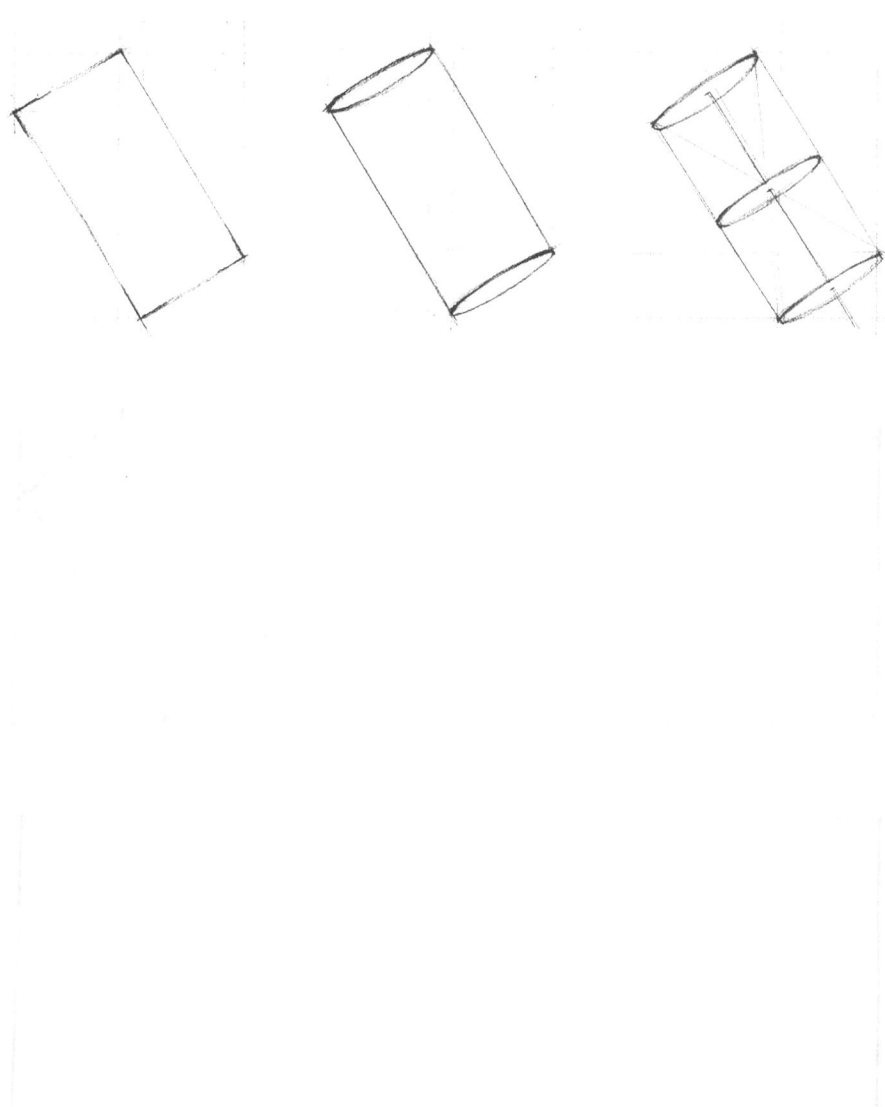

ADD VOLUME TO A DRAWING

This exercise is a great way to take a complex shape and envision it as more manageable parts. What geometric solids do you think the artist used to draw the teapot below? The answer is shown opposite: a sphere, cylinder, and cone. In the contour provided, place the geometric solids where you think they belong to add volume. What shape can be modified to make the handle?

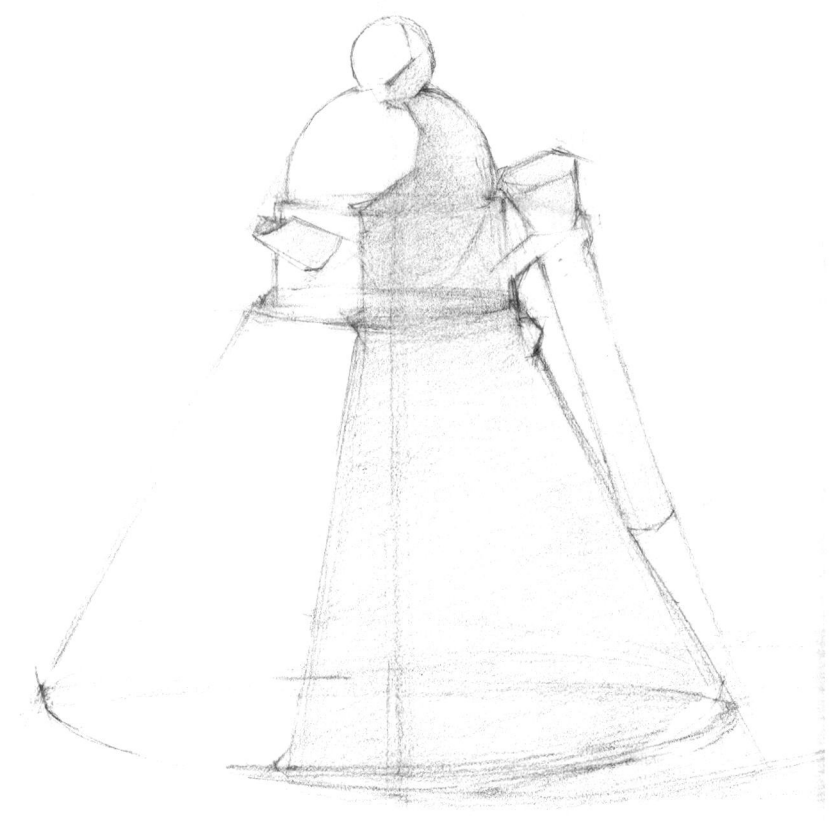

John Zadrozny, *Teapot Demonstration*, 2017, graphite on paper, 12 x 10 inches (30.5 x 25.4 cm), Aristides Atelier

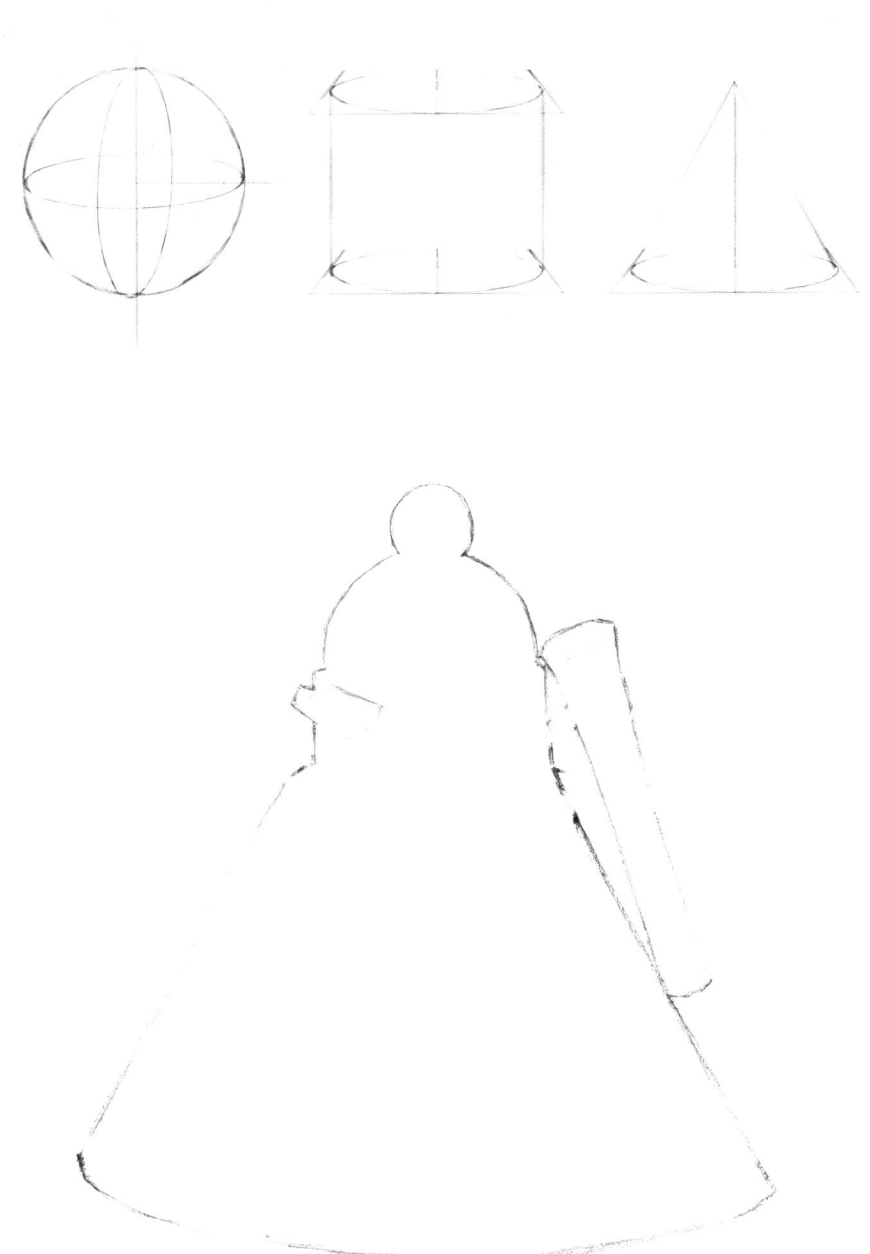

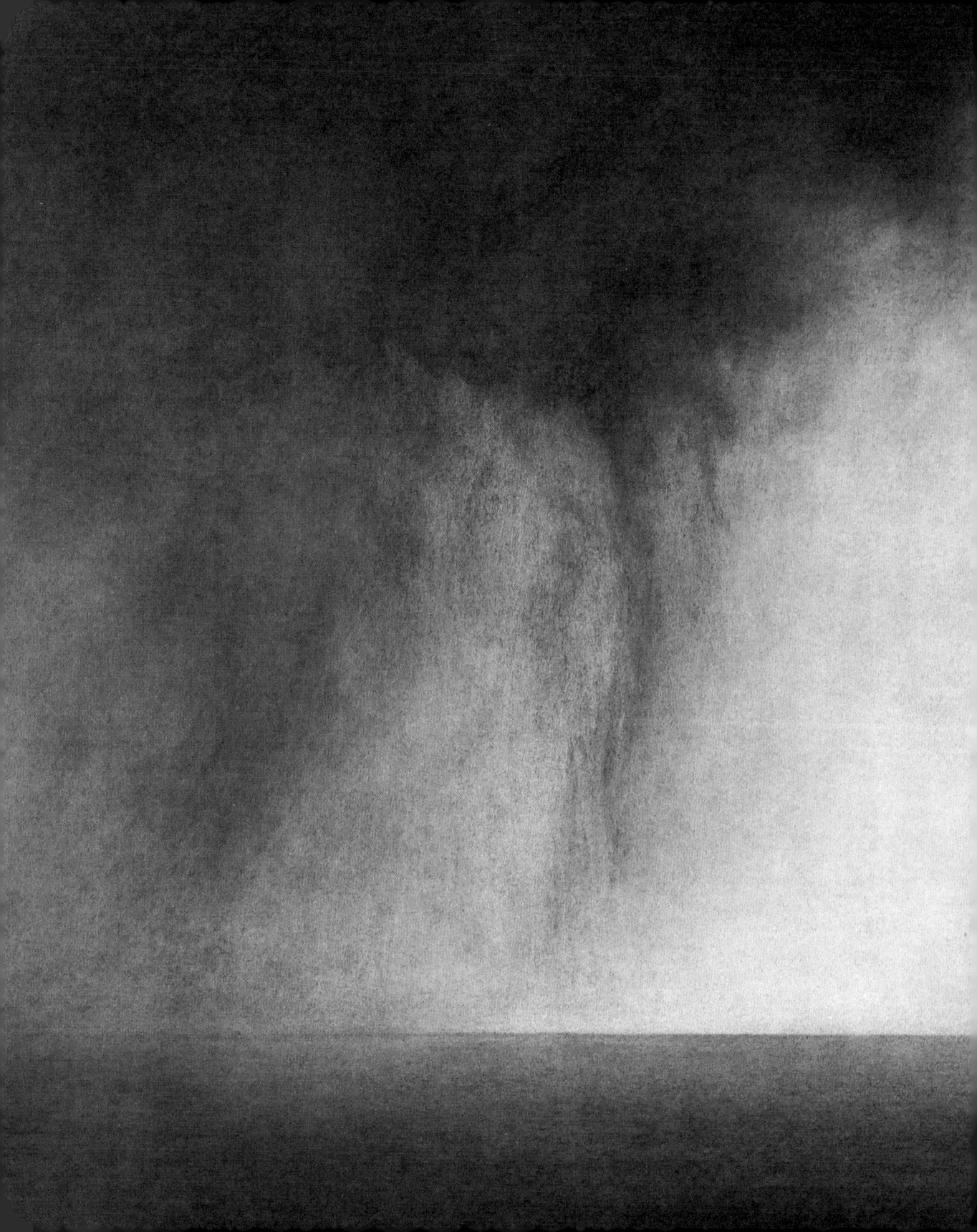

FOUR

VALUE

Hold to this principle that the greatest drawing, the greatest expression,
the greatest completion, the sense of all contained, lies in what can be done
through the larger masses and the larger gestures.

—ROBERT HENRI, *THE ART SPIRIT*

I get easily overwhelmed in a pharmacy, with the bright lights and shelves stretching for miles in all directions. Between the competing stacks of products and the people in the aisles, I don't know where to look. By contrast, any great work of art leads our eye with a careful arrangement of edges, lights, and darks. For example, if there is a crowd of people in a scene by Rembrandt, it is not uncommon for the figures in the back to be darker and less focused, the artwork gaining in clarity and contrast as we approach the principal focal point. Sometimes in life, too, we choose to control attention, such as by lighting a candle at dinner and turning off the overhead lights.

Value, or tone, is one of the most important aspects of drawing yet also the most hidden in real life. It is the light and dark that underlies our world in color. Value is easy to understand if you think of a black-and-white photograph, instead of a color one, and its many variations of gray.

The common artistic practice of working from photographs often results in an accidental mimicking of the chaos of the pharmacy. The speckling of lights and darks seen in the photo is allowed into the art, distracting us from the focal point (if there is one) and confusing viewers. Rather than simply copying the random speckling of lights and darks seen in life, we must simplify the countless small value changes into larger groupings, creating an abstract design (even if your artwork is realistic). This *value composition* is critical, yet hidden from the viewer—just as the architect's blueprint is hidden when we look at a building.

OPPOSITE: Nicolas De Jesus, *Mare Incognitum: Rain Squall* (detail), 2015, 22 x 22 inches (56 x 56 cm), charcoal on cotton paper, private collection

Mapping value

To add value, we start, as always, by working large to small (or general to specific), thinking about the largest possible tonal shapes before giving our attention to more nuanced gradations.

The process of simplifying value is called "mapping" and involves distilling many values into an average tonality. At its simplest, this can be done with only two values—black and white—as in Sandra Bolton's ink drawing of a Caravaggio, shown opposite. More often, we play with four or five values to create a compelling composition. Through value mapping, we capture the effect of a scene without the detail, like something caught out of the corner of one's eye. We simplify the countless values seen in life into large masses; the bigger the better.

When people refer to a drawing as "overworked," they are rarely critiquing the amount of time spent on it, but rather, noticing that the drawing has lost the clarity of big shapes. The values and edges have become muddled. Practically speaking, it may mean that there are lights in your darks and dark notes in the lights. When working from life, we must learn to control the viewer's attention by simplifying, knowing what to subordinate to keep the picture working as a single, powerful image. This is essential to creating a memorable work of art that reads well from a distance.

Generally, we map values at two stages in the drawing process: when finding our shadow shapes, and when we do sketches or thumbnail studies (small, quick drawings that allow us to see if our ideas work before investing time in a larger piece).

To map value, start by lightly toning the shadow shapes in your block-in. As you do this, notice how you can merge these shapes with others of similar value to create connections throughout your drawing. You want to create the largest groupings possible so that your drawing is made of several value blocks rather than hundreds of incidental tonal relationships.

The core shadow (the dividing line between your lights and your shadows) takes on a stronger and more defined role. Study the shadow line dividing the light and dark in Melissa Messer's block-in on page 81. See how she used straight, broken little lines for their edges? Each jagged change in line direction along the edge indicates a change of form, describing the surface of the object to the viewer.

When an edge is located *within* a shadow, or in another dark area, let it dissolve into the larger shape. For example, the contour of a shirt can become lost in the tone of the background. These decisions are not arbitrary but are made by studying your subject. The process of dissolving some lines and sharpening others is called lost-and-found edges. Every drawing

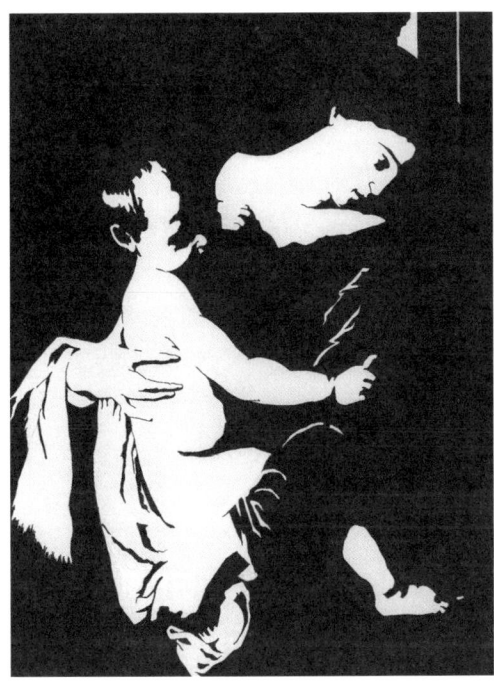

has a range of edges, from a few very sharp edges, decreasing in contrast until some areas have no edges at all.

Here are some quick tips on mapping:

- Squint at your master drawing or real-life subject. This blocks light from your retina, making it easier to filter out details and preserve the sense of seeing your object for the first time.

- Map your object into four or five value shapes, grouping them by tone and subordinating the details within. Think about these large shapes as puzzle pieces or continents on a map, with the edges as coastlines.

- Lightly shade your shapes into fairly uniform blocks of value before building richer mid-tones and darks.

- Stand back from your drawing to see it from a distance. Can any of the shapes be made simpler? Can the edgework be more descriptive?

ABOVE, LEFT: Sandra Bolton, *Copy of Detail from Caravaggio's* Madonna di Loreto, 2015, ink on paper, 10 ½ x 8 inches (26.7 x 20.3 cm)

Sandra Bolton practiced simplifying value into large shapes by grouping tones either as black or white, using a detail from Caravaggio's masterwork as inspiration.

ABOVE, RIGHT: Deborah Lloyd, *Into the Unknown*, 2017, charcoal and pastel on paper, 8 ½ x 8 inches (21.6 x 20.3 cm). Image courtesy of Art Renewal Center

Out of the countless variations of tone seen in a real sky, road, and car, Deborah Lloyd has distilled the largest possible value groupings, keeping the shapes broad and avoiding detail except in the contour of the trees against the sky.

MAP SHADOWS WITH TONE

In *Pears on a Vine*, below, notice how the artist kept the shadow shapes broad and linked together, yet the edges between the light and dark are well seen and nuanced. Practice adding tone by lightly shading the shadow shapes in the block-in, opposite.

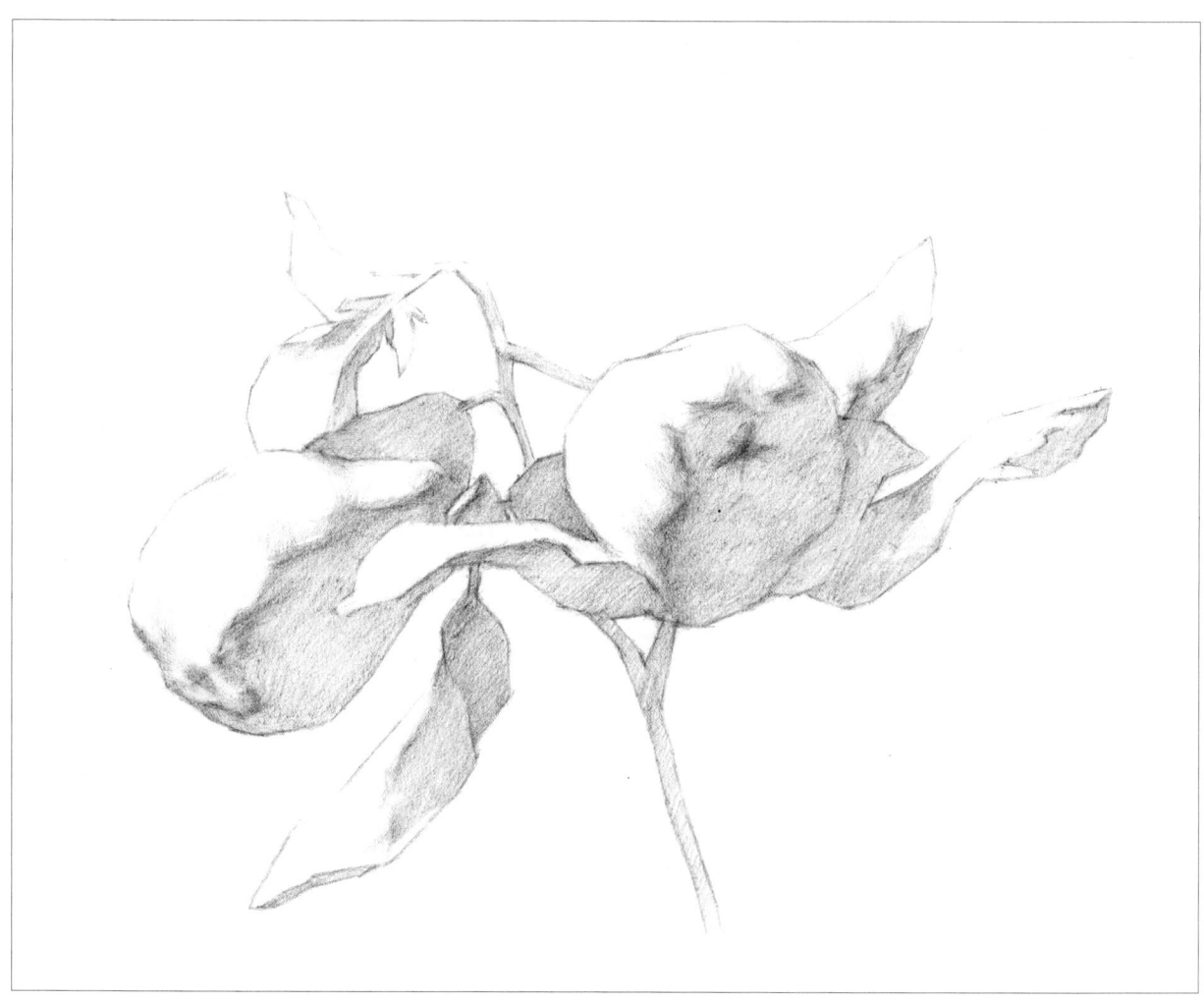

Melissa Messer, *Pears on a Vine*, 2017, 9 x 12 inches (22.9 x 30.5 cm), Aristides Atelier

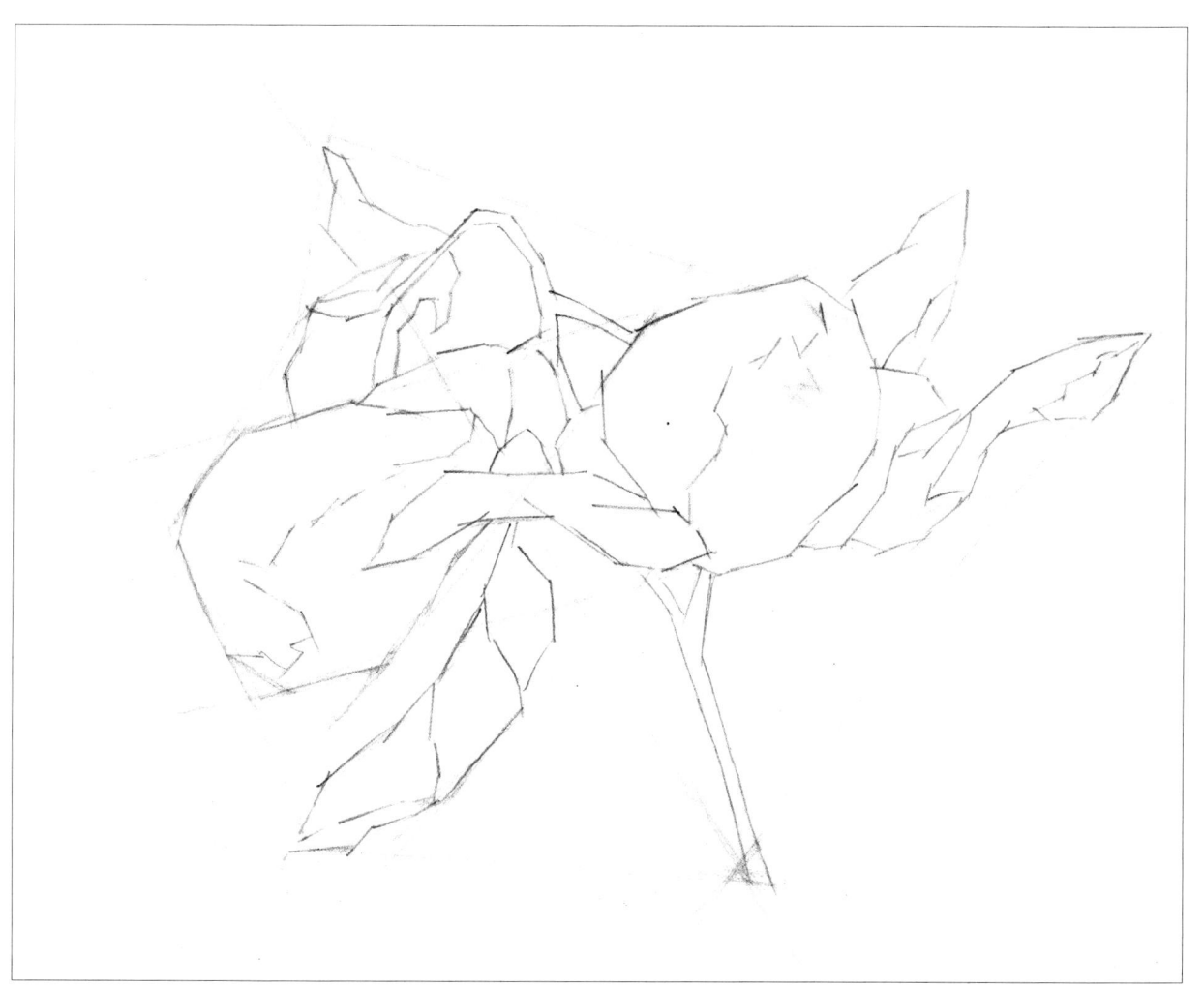

PRACTICE MAPPING VALUE

Here, we see the full sequence, from refined block-in to initial value map (opposite, top) to final rendering of value (below). Notice how some edges, such as of the center and right apples, have disappeared into the larger shadow shape. Practice mapping value by lightly toning the shadow shapes in the block-in to re-create the finished sketch.

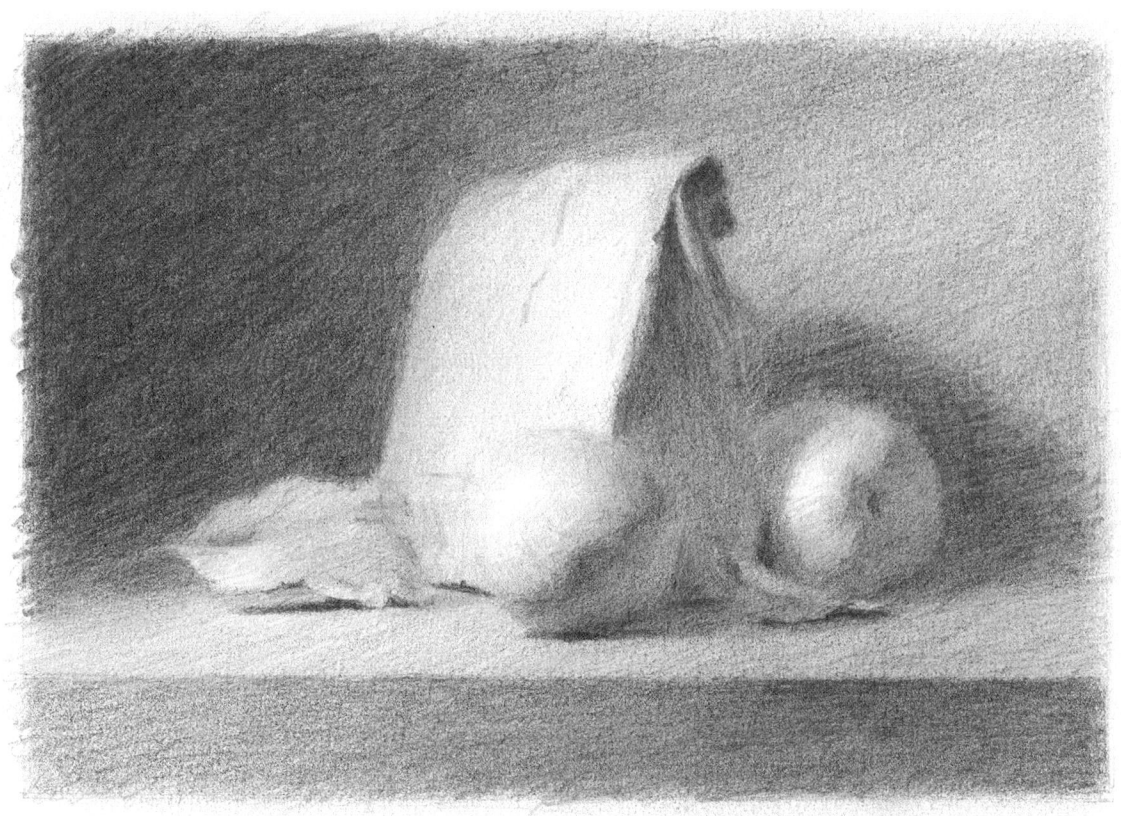

Paul Rosiak, *Still Life Demonstration*, 2017, graphite on paper, 9 x 12 inches (22.9 x 30.5 cm), Aristides Atelier

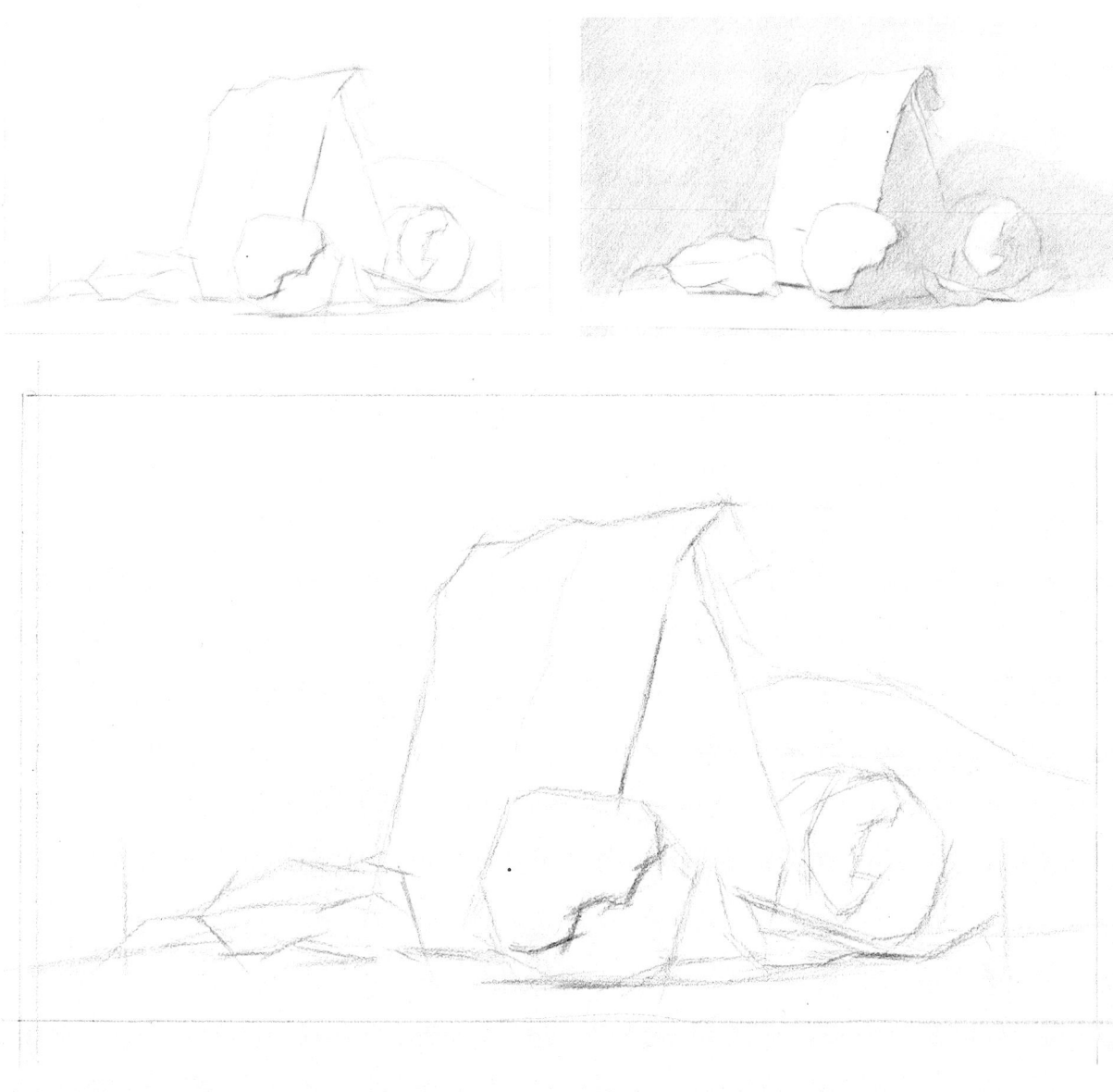

MAKE TONAL DRAWINGS

Sktech the drawings here and on pages 86–87. Start by finding the height and width of the whole image and creating a rectangle the same size for your drawing on the blank space opposite. Block in the general angles that describe the shapes, as you did for the lemon and pitcher on page 53. Next, lightly tone your shapes, grouping and simplifying as much as possible. At this point, compare your drawing with the original. If it captures the general effect, continue by pushing the darks in your drawing and bring to a finish.

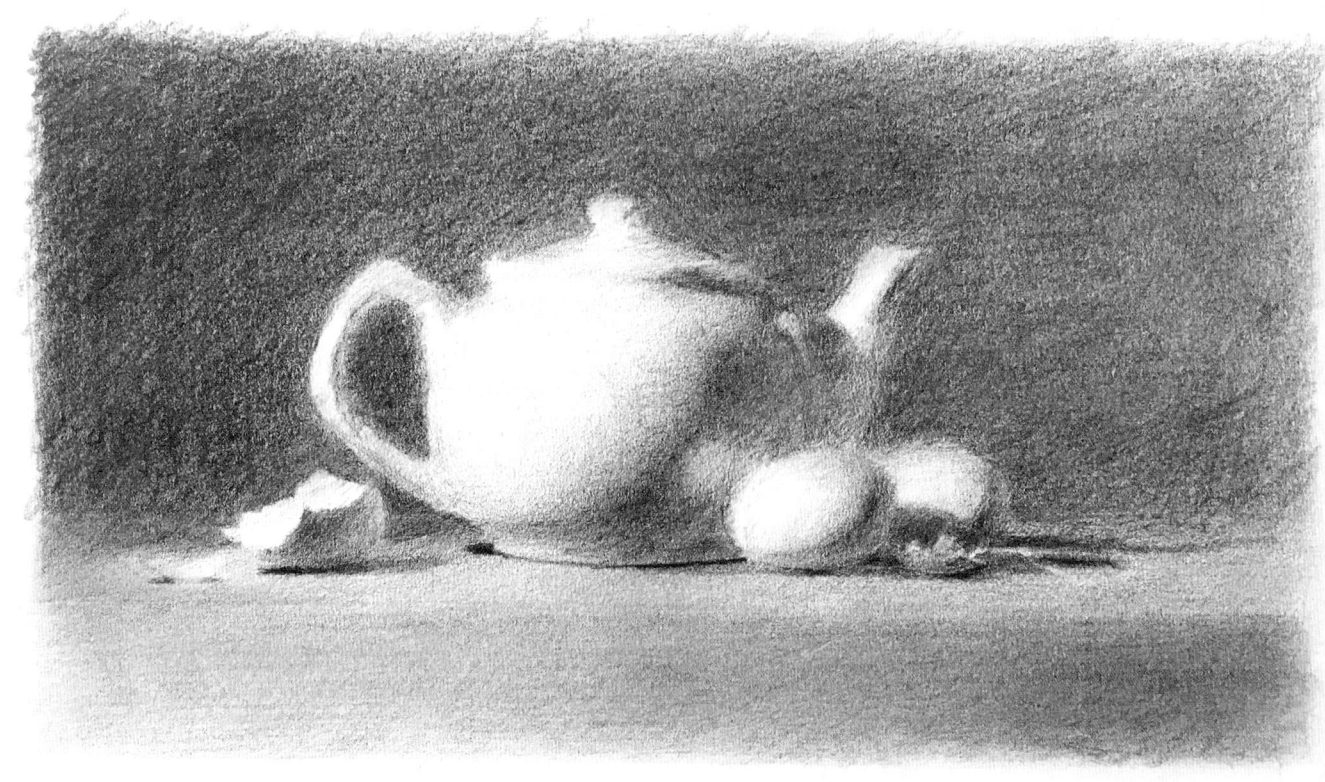

Paul Rosiak, *Study of a Teapot,* 2017, charcoal on paper, 6 x 8 inches (15.2 x 20.3 cm), collection unknown, Aristides Atelier

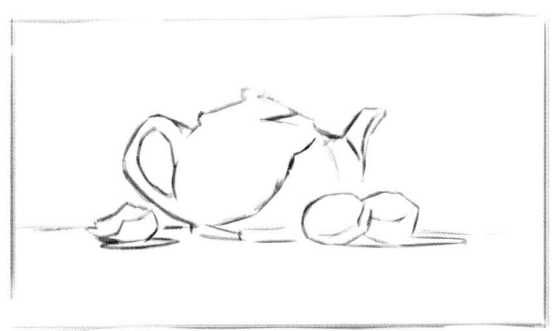 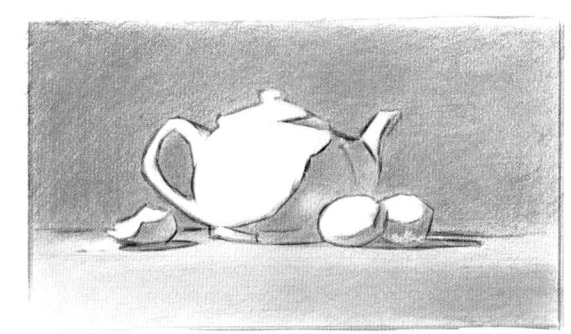

SKETCH A LANDSCAPE

Sketch this drawing on the page opposite. Block in the general lines and shapes as you did on page 53. Next, lightly tone your shapes into large value blocks. Flick your eye between your drawing and the original to check for accuracy. If you have captured the general effect, continue by pushing the darks and finding specific details, like the railroad tracks and shrubs, to bring it to a finish.

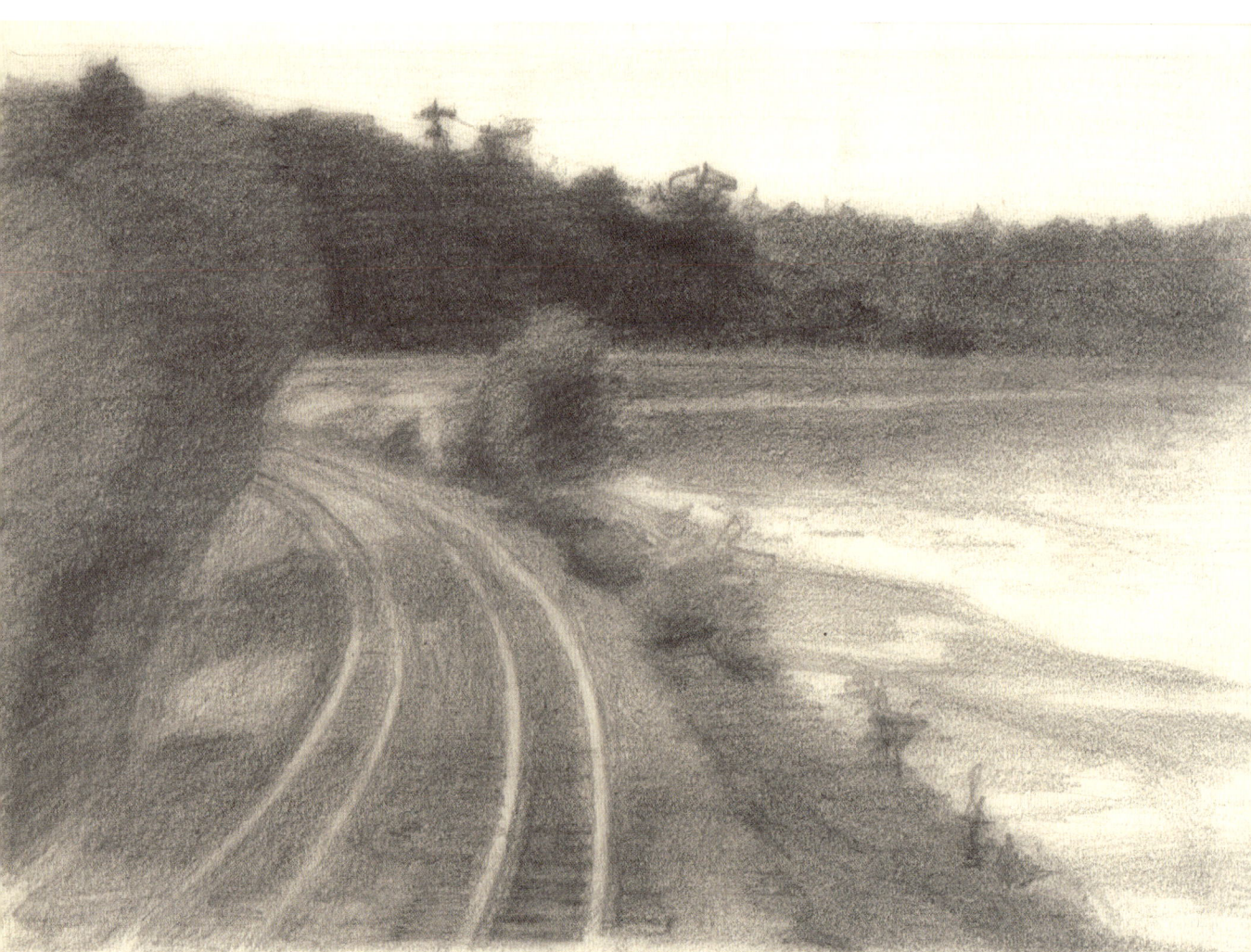

Zoey Frank, *Carkeek*, 2017, graphite on paper, 8 x 10 ½ inches (20.3 x 26.7 cm)

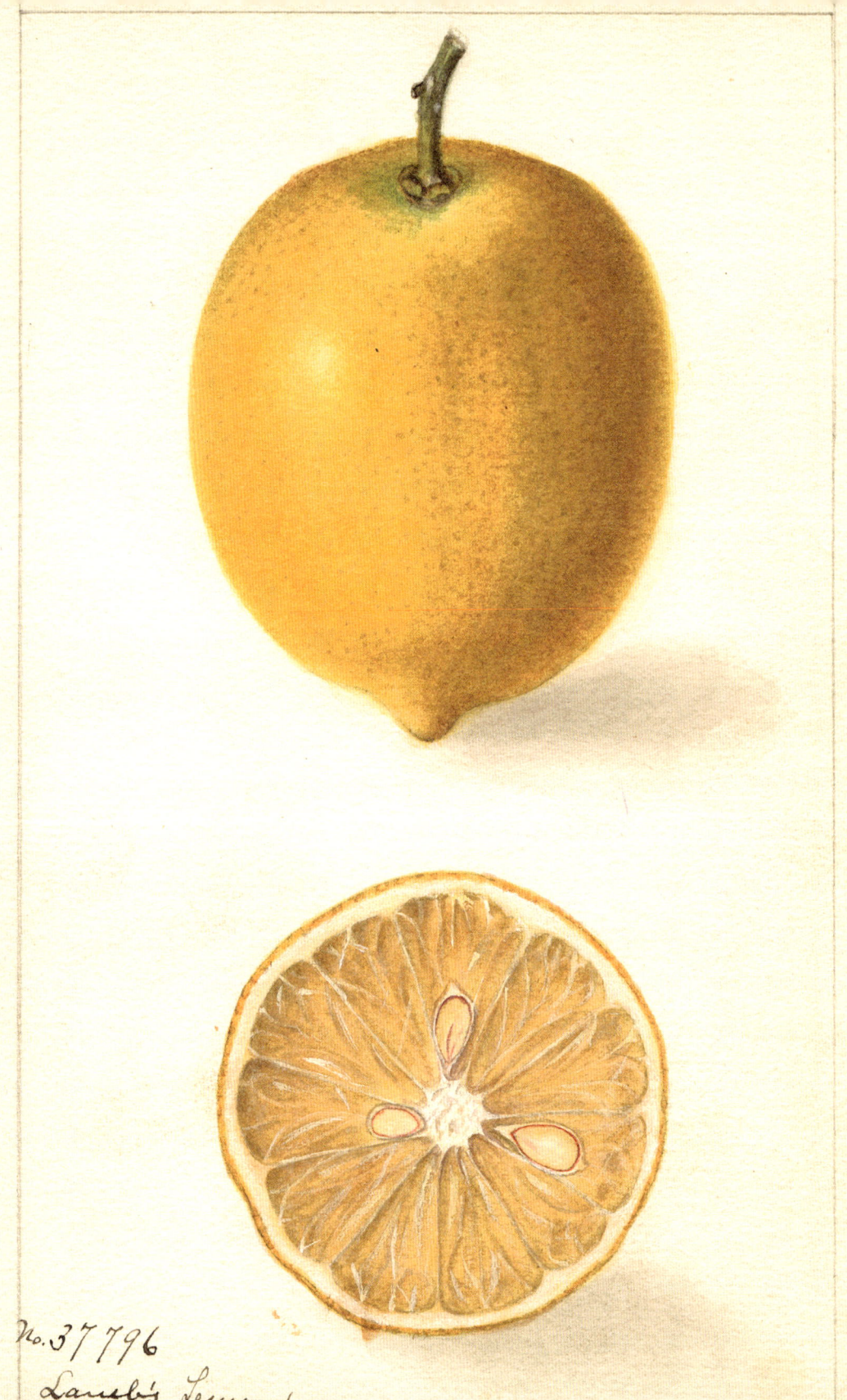

No. 37796
Lamb's Lemon

FIVE

FORM

This book can go under the microscope. You'd find life under the glass,
streaming past in infinite profusion. The more pores, the more truthfully recorded
details of life per square inch you can get on a sheet of paper....
—RAY BRADBURY, *FAHRENHEIT 451*

It has been raining in Seattle for months when a blast of evening light rakes through my house, revealing that the clean surfaces were just an illusion. Small forms are now exposed: the scratches on the floor, the nicks and scrapes on chairs, tiny spots of dust floating through the air. Dirt and imperfection—so hated by housekeepers, but loved by artists who enjoy looking past cold perfection to study light hitting real forms. This texture documents the life of an object, a sense of place, and a life deeply inhabited and etched into a surface. The belief that one spot is unlike anywhere else in the world, and unique from any other time, lies at the heart of form drawing.

Until now we have been thinking exclusively about large lines and shapes, which provide a solid foundation for our drawings. In chapter 4, we thought about value abstractly as flat shapes, but now we will think about it literally as we observe actual light hitting an object.

I am more of a "big shapes and dark lines" kind of person who favors impact over subtlety, so as a student I found the hours learning to render tone very difficult. (*Rendering* is the finishing of our drawing in full value, often referring to the gradual application of tone used to make something look three-dimensional.) It takes time for our eyes to acclimate to seeing these twilight gradations of value that hover in the midtone area of our subject. In fact, it is rare for non-artists to see them at all. But over time, I grew to appreciate the slowing down and deeper seeing that comes from this practice. One cannot create the illusion of volume without gradation. The more gradation there is, the rounder the surface of your object appears.

OPPOSITE: Ellen Isham Schutt, *Citrus Lemon*, 1907, watercolor on paper, size unknown, U.S. Department of Agriculture Pomological Watercolor Collection, Rare and Special Collections, National Agricultural Library

Rendering form

When artists set up a light source to illuminate a subject, we often choose classic form-revealing lighting. This is light that comes from above at an angle, leaving the subject about two-thirds lit and one-third in shadow. Most of us prefer this to front-facing light, which casts few, if any, shadows, or backlighting, which places the subject entirely in shadow (except perhaps for a rim of light around the edge). Light coming from below appears sinister, illuminating the usual shadow planes and casting normally lit planes into darkness. While any light source can be used for art, the study of form is best begun with classic lighting that reveals the surface shapes of a subject.

Your drawing is ready for form when you have clearly mapped out and lightly toned the shadow shapes, as covered in the last chapter. Now we will gradually build up the richness of the values in that drawing.

Form drawing is an exercise in patience and the subtle rendering between dark and light. The more halftones you place, the rounder the surface will look, because halftones describe a changing surface. It's the difference between a ball and a circle, a portrait and a playing card. When doing the exercises in this section, build up your tones slowly and lightly, in layers, and your investment of time will be well rewarded. Form drawing is a love of weight, of the small, unique things that surround us every day. And so we find the truth in the words of Mary Oliver: "Attention is the beginning of devotion."

OPPOSITE: Jordan Sokol, *Model 1925*, 2017, charcoal pencil and white chalk on hand-toned paper, 29 ¼ x 28 ½ inches (74.3 x 72.4 cm)

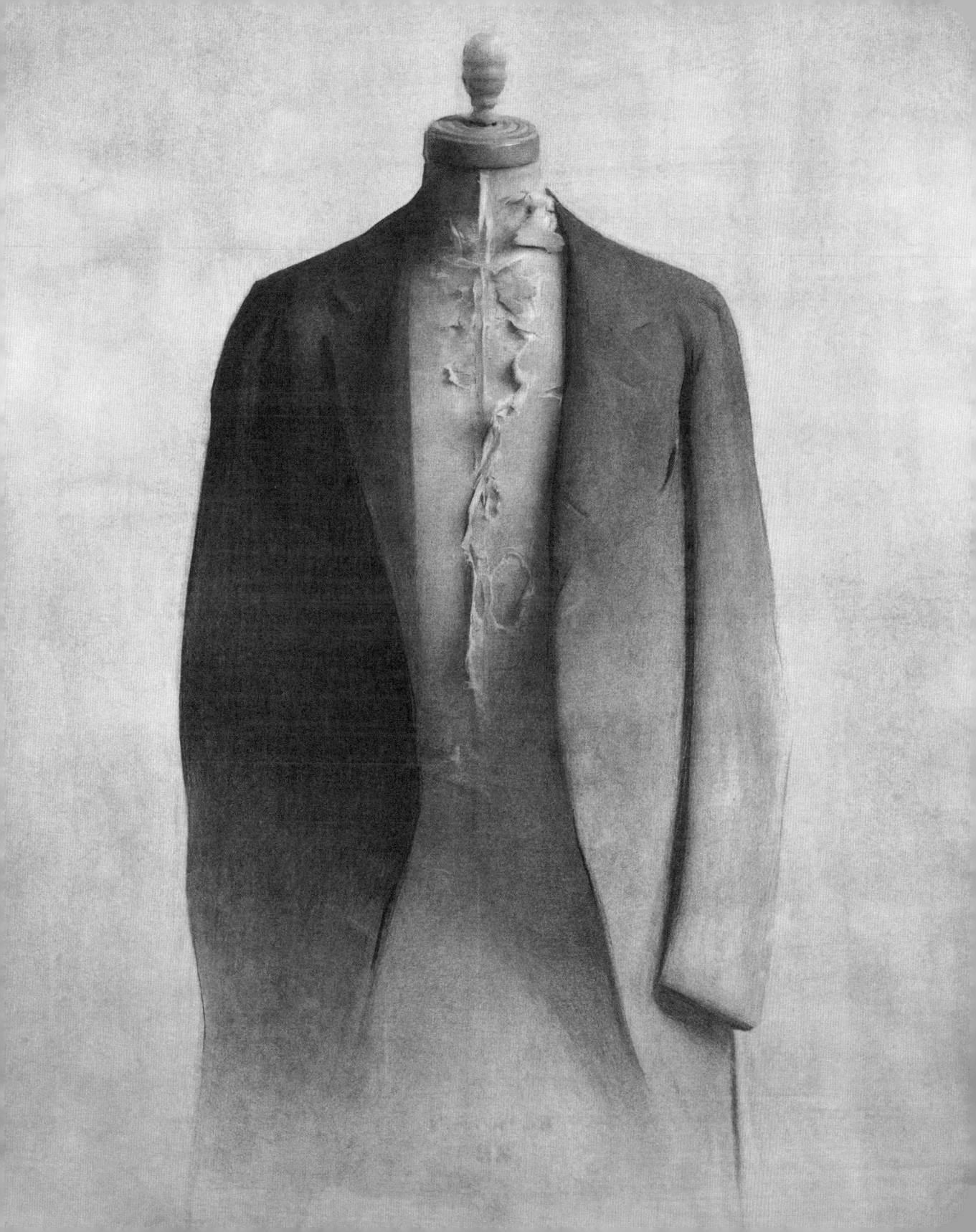

Classic order of light and the step scale

Artists often practice rendering tone with a *step scale,* or grayscale, a row or column of value squares. White is at one end of the scale and black is at the other end. These value steps roughly correspond to the stages seen when light hits an object, accounting for light, midtone, and shadow.

White represents the highest highlight, the glowing glare spot of light bouncing off your object. The next several squares capture gradated tone, from highest light to the local (average tone under normal lighting conditions) value of my light object. The next few values show the midtones as the light hitting my object begins to turn away from the light source and toward the shadow. The core, or darkest part, of the shadow is captured by the darker tones in your scale, depending on how dark or light your object is. Black is the darkest dark, the undercut of your object and sometimes cast shadow. Of course, this is a vague ideal. Your actual situation will be represented by cascading values, from light to dark, that describe the surface of your object, all affected by the direction of the light, the color of your object, and the environment it is placed within.

When creating a value step scale, go slowly. Don't try to get the exact tone in the first pass. Build up layers of graphite or charcoal to get rich, controlled, even layers of tone. You'll know you are getting it right when the same square appears both lighter and darker depending on what it is next to. This optical illusion (called *simultaneous contrast*) shows us how the same value appears to change depending on what you place adjacent to it.

The nine values of a step scale, from light to dark. Practice filling in the bottom step scale yourself.

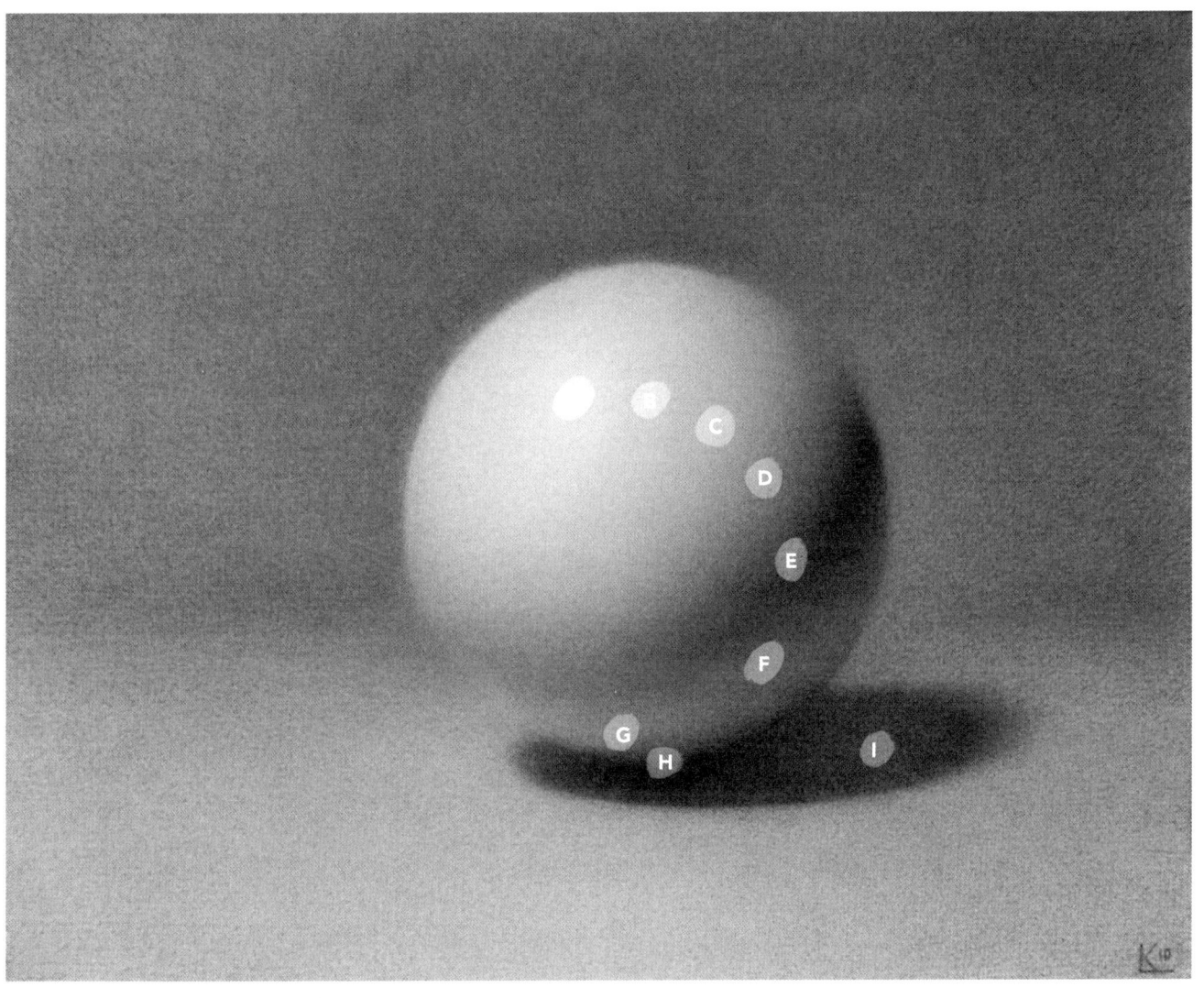

It is helpful to know the anatomy of how light and shadow hits an object. See if you can identify these areas in other drawings in this chapter.

A. Highlight

B. Local light

C. Light halftone

D. Dark halftone

E. Core shadow

F. Body of the shadow

G. Reflected light

H. Dark accent

I. Cast shadow

DRAW A VALUE SPHERE

Sktech this sphere in the blank space opposite. Start by drawing a circle. Add a crescent moon for the core shadow shape and a horizon line for the back edge of the table. Lightly shade the shadow (crescent shape) on the sphere and the cast shadow on the ground plane before placing your background. As shown in stage three, render your halftones perpendicular to your core shadow, getting lighter as you move toward the highlight (like a mini step scale). Finish by methodically rendering the halftones. (If you wish, you can leave out the background.)

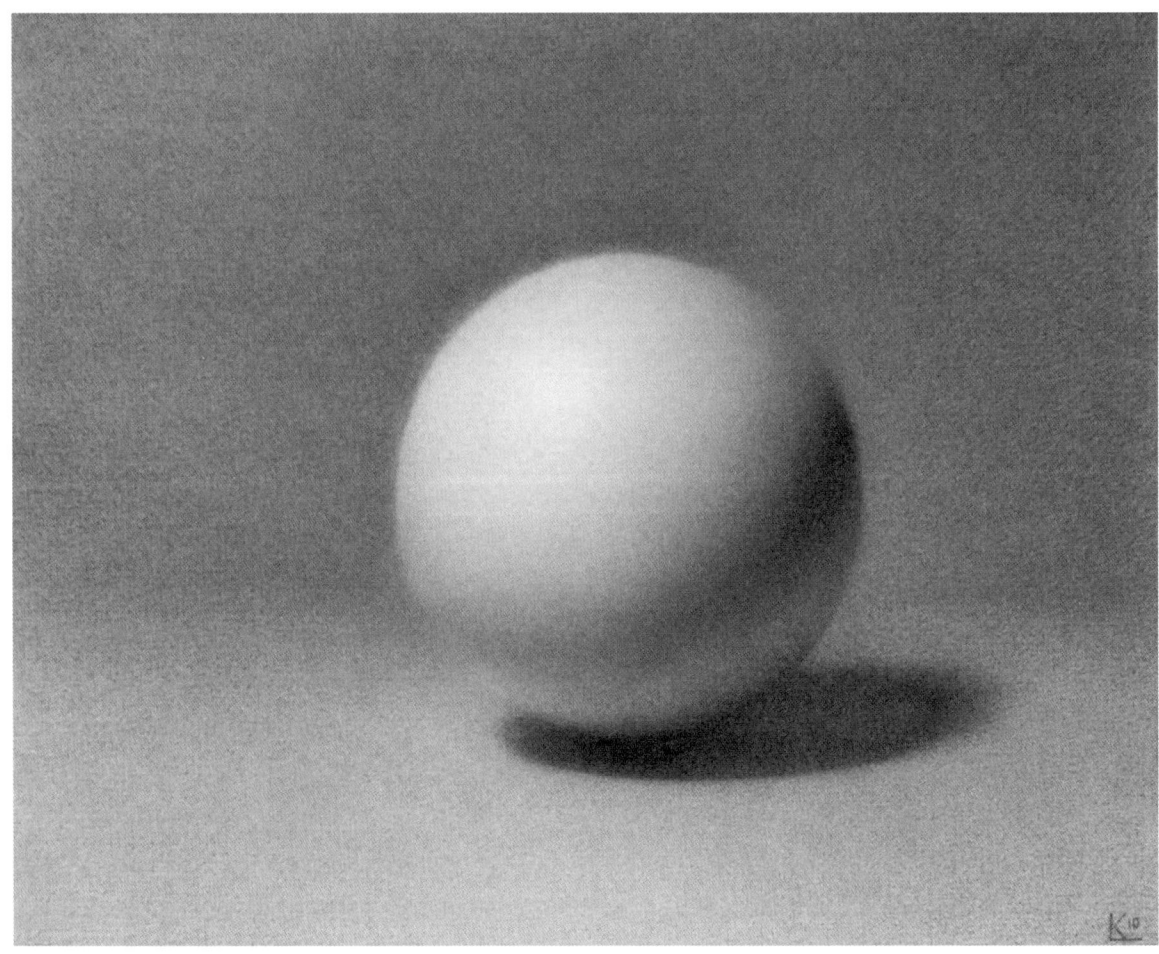

Damien Leeds, *Sphere*, 2010, charcoal on paper, 8 x 10 inches (20.3 x 25.4 cm), Aristides Atelier

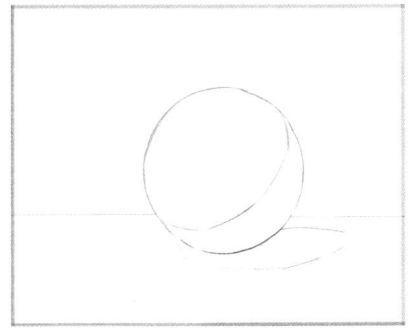 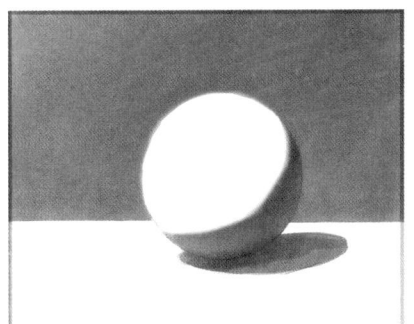 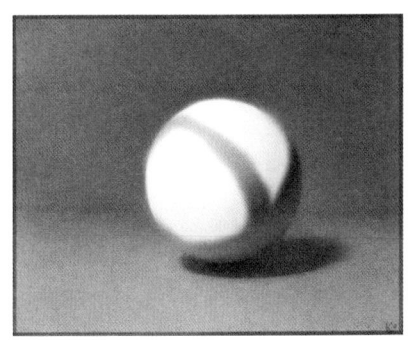

DRAW FORM

Sketch the drawings here and on pages 98–100, applying the lessons learned from the value sphere. For each, sketch a light block-in in the space provided, then map the values and render form. You can choose to copy the drawings as shown or arrange another apple, pear, or egg on a table in front of you, using a single light source on your subject.

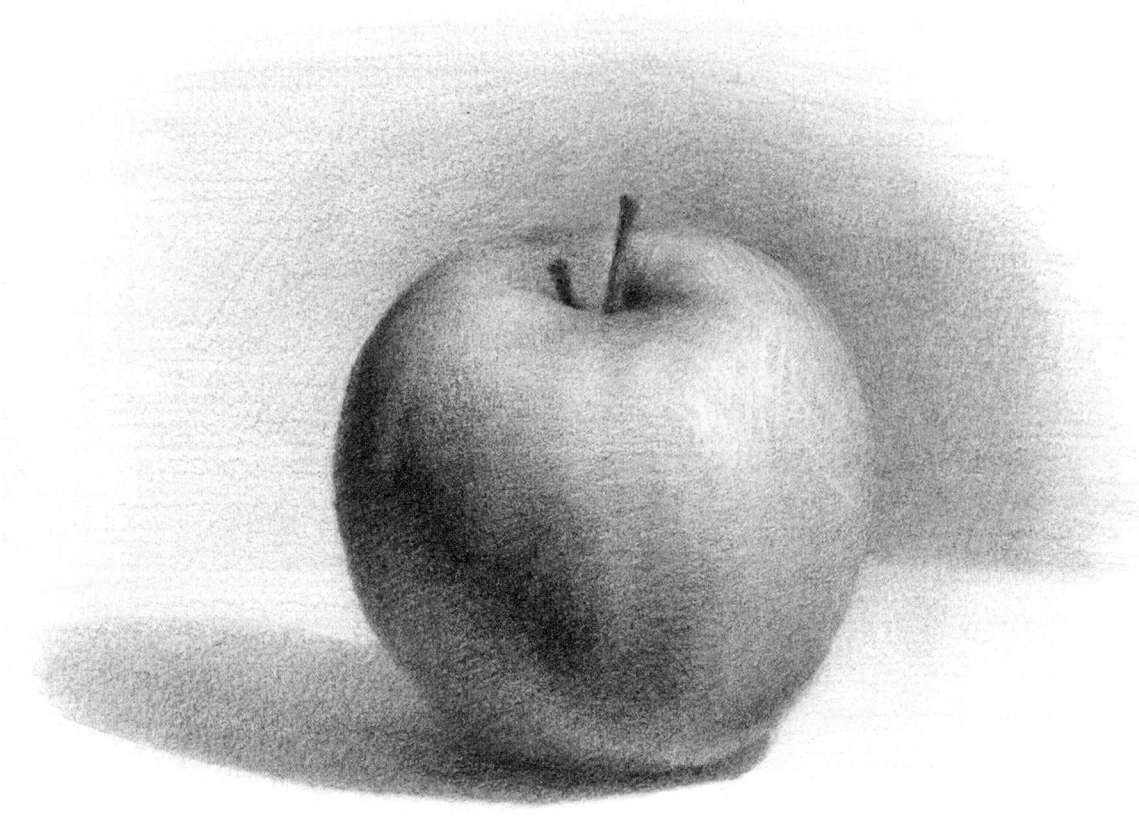

Grace Flott, *Apple Demonstration*, 2018, graphite on paper, 8 x 10 inches (20.3 x 25.4 cm), Aristides Atelier

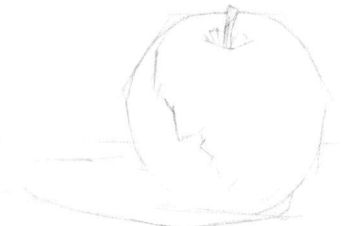 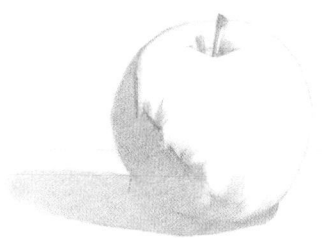 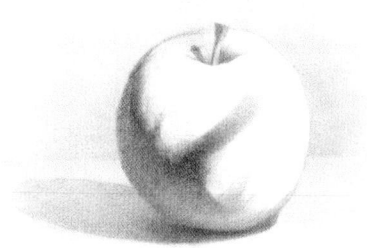

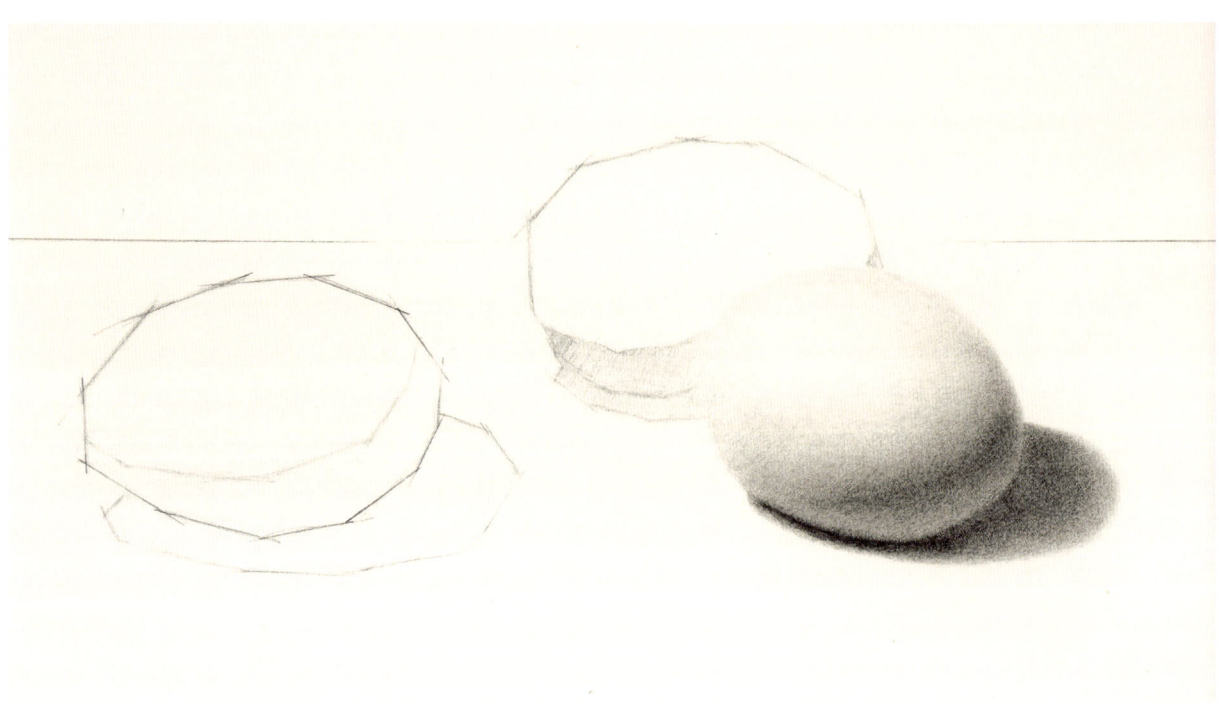

Robin Warner, *Eggs Demonstration* (detail), 2017, graphite on paper, 8 x 10 inches (20.3 x 25.4 cm), Aristides Atelier

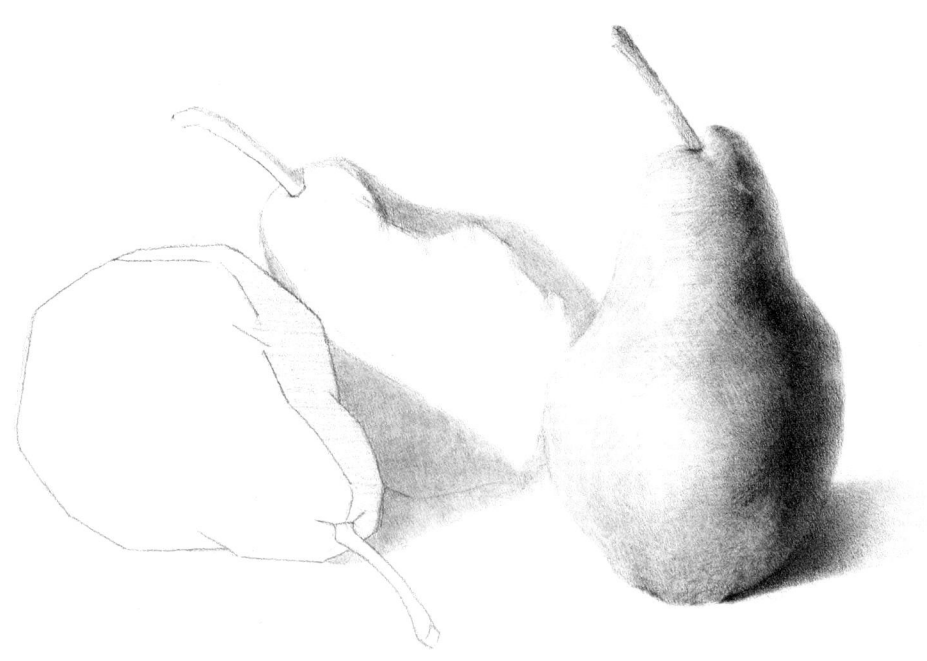

Karen Poole, *Pear Demonstration* (detail), 2017, graphite on paper, 8 x 10 inches (20.3 x 25.4 cm), Aristides Atelier

Charles Bargue, *Charles Bargue: Drawing Course,* Plate I, 26. *Child's leg, rear view (Jambe d'enfant),* lithograph, 28 x 24 inches (71.1 x 61 cm), from *Charles Bargue: Drawing Course,* Aristides Atelier

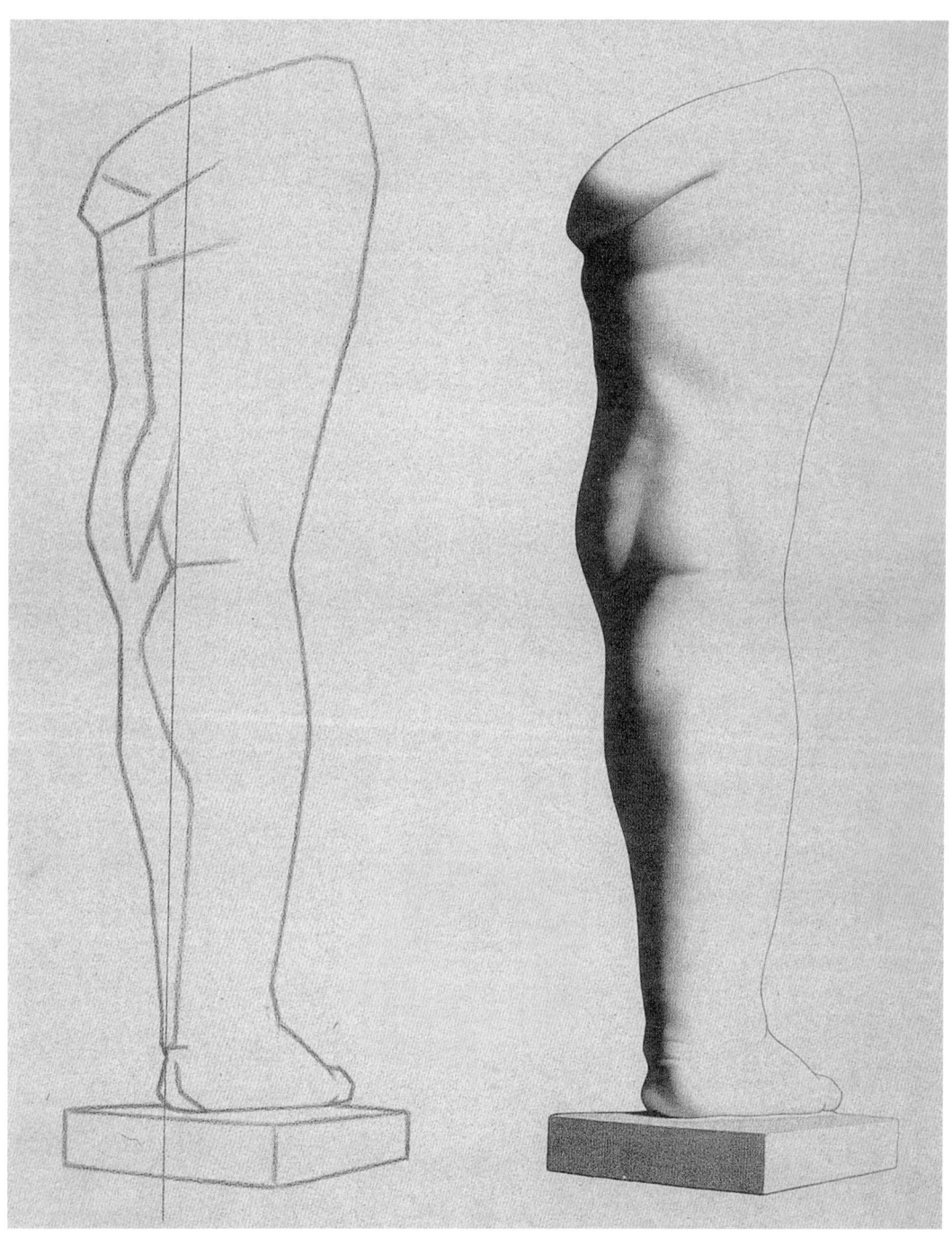

Copy both the block-in and finished drawing of Charles Bargue's *Child's leg* in the space below. Alternatively, create one drawing by using the block-in as the first step before moving on to the finished rendering.

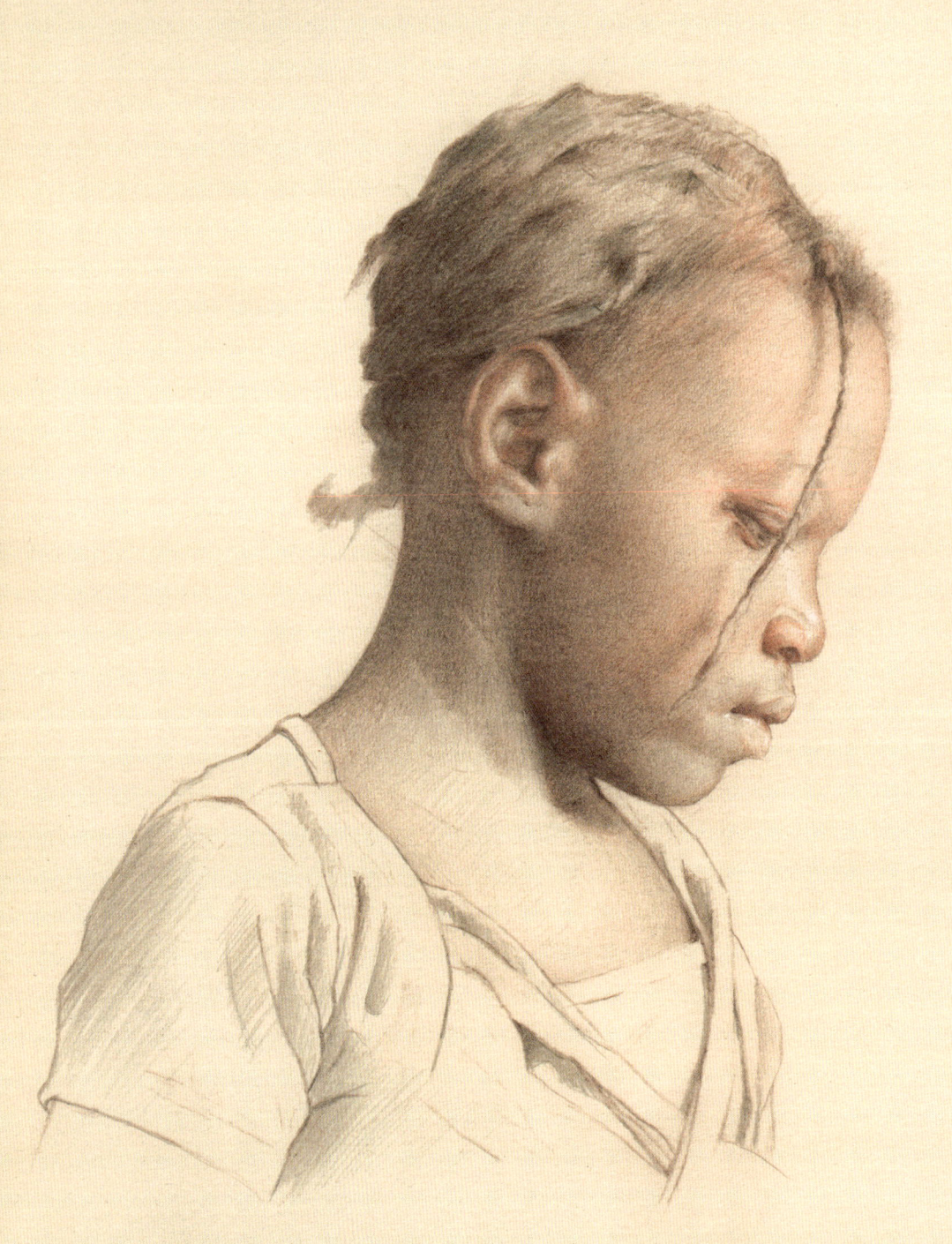

SIX

PORTRAITS

The moment one gives close attention to anything, even a blade of grass,
it becomes a mysterious, awesome, indescribably magnificent world in itself.
—HENRY MILLER

One day, I was in the Seattle airport drinking a coffee in a chair perfectly placed behind a potted plant, affording me a quiet spot to wait for my flight as the crowds passed by. At one point, a man in a wheelchair rolled by, and just as he passed, he turned and we locked eyes. (He didn't look *at* me but *into* me, if that makes sense.) It all happened in a second. Yet, later that night, of the thousands of anonymous faces that had gone past, his was the only one I remembered. Now, years later, I still remember him; the connection made in an instant was that strong.

To be seen is a powerful gift, closely aligned with expressions of friendship and even love. Because of this, drawing a face is often emotionally charged. The face conveys both the emotional and intellectual life of a person. We look to the face to see ourselves, hoping to find out if we are fitting in or being understood. There is a tyranny to drawing a face: everyone knows what it looks like, and the margin for error is tiny.

Because of the intensity of our emotions and everyone's familiarity with faces, drawing people is difficult. To draw a portrait well, we need, first, a measure of emotional distance for objectivity: to see our subject (or subjects) separate from his or her function or our experience. So, when approaching a drawing or painting, think about it as a head study, rather than a portrait. Changing the way we think takes the pressure off having to capture the soul of the model in addition to the likeness. We can set a more attainable goal, all the while realizing that a truly good head study often contains all the elements of an insightful portrait.

Next, realize that the principles of drawing are generally the same no matter what your subject is, be it a tree, figure, or still life. You are still going to block in the basic shapes and then refine them, adding volume, mapping values, and rendering form, generally working from large to small forms.

OPPOSITE: Gregory Mortenson, *Little Braid*, 2015, pencil on paper, 11 x 9 inches (28 x 23 cm)

Understanding the shape of the head

The features of the face, especially the eyes and mouth, are actually the tiniest areas of the head. If we start by drawing those small shapes we skip the principles of good drawing and will not achieve a solid head study. After all, we were not constructed in a piecemeal manner. The best way to draw the head repeats the logic we have followed throughout this sketchbook: general to specific. It is the large, hidden shape of the skull that determines the shape and proportion of the head. Likeness is almost always found in these big shapes.

The human skull can be simplified into two bony masses: the oval cranial shape of the head and the angular mandible (or jawbone). Take a moment to feel the shape of your own head, how it swells into a rounded form at the back and flattens in the front where the features sit. This is often shorthanded by artists into a circle with a squared, V-shaped wedge for the jaw. This is a flexible model that both accounts for anatomy and can be used for quick placement. The more commonly used drawing of a circle for the head is too simple.

Next, artists often imagine that this rounded shape of our heads can fit into a box. Rounded shapes have no orientation; it is impossible to see how things are tipping and tilting. But if we formalize the head into a boxy shape with clear planes, we have something to draw. This artistic hallucination is a remarkably useful tool on which to build our portrait.

To find the box for the head, follow these steps. Keep in mind that these are only your notations. The viewer will feel the strength of the alignments but never know that you thought of the head first as a box.

1. Place your hand flat against your face, with your fingertips touching your hairline and your palm at your chin (or as close as you can). That is the front face plane.
2. Place your hands over your ears. Can you feel the flatness around your temples and the edge of your jaw? That becomes the sides of your box.
3. The rounded back of the head gets flattened to become a flat plane at the back of the box.
4. The underside of the jaw indicates the bottom plane.

Keep in mind that the box is only a visual aid to help you understand what you see, much the way we used geometric solids in the chapter on volume. The box should be implied but never seen in your final drawings.

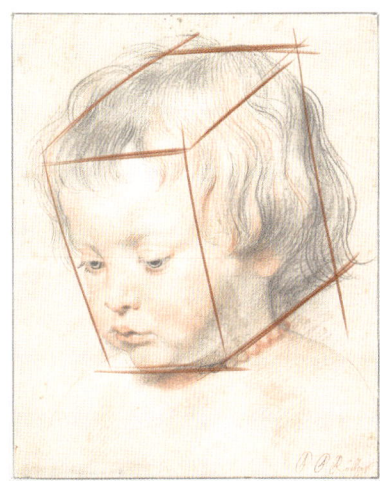

1

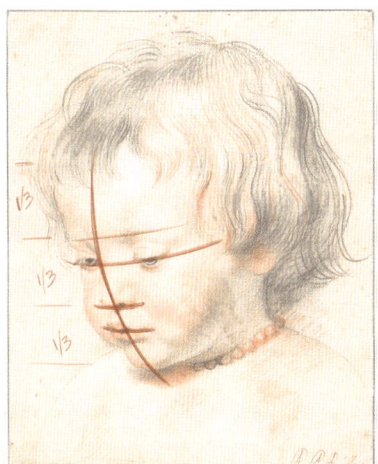

2

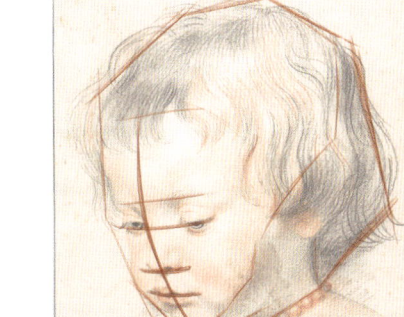

3

DRAW THE SCAFFOLDING

Follow the steps below to draw scaffolding on the image of Rubens's *Nicolaas Rubens Wearing a Coral Necklace*, below.

1. Draw a box around the head.

2. Draw the centerline of the face, and the scaffolding for the eyebrows, eyes, nose, and mouth.

3. Add the block-in lines of the head, along with the shadow shape. Now you have the full scaffolding of the head.

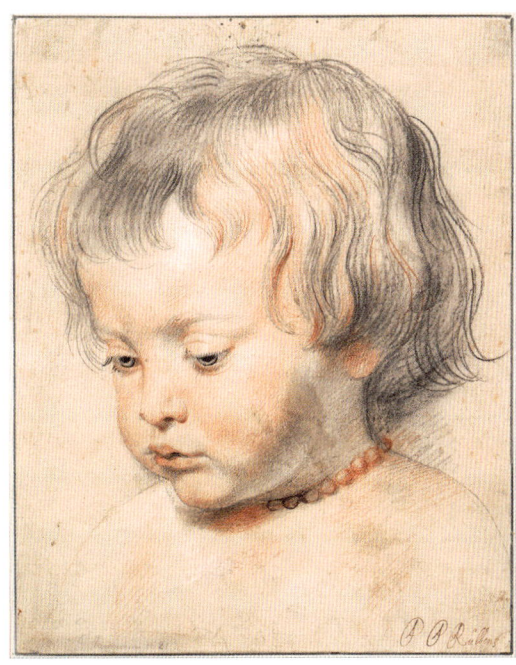

Peter Paul Rubens, *Nicolaas Rubens Wearing a Coral Necklace*, 1619, white chalk, black chalk, and sanguine on paper, Albertina, Vienna

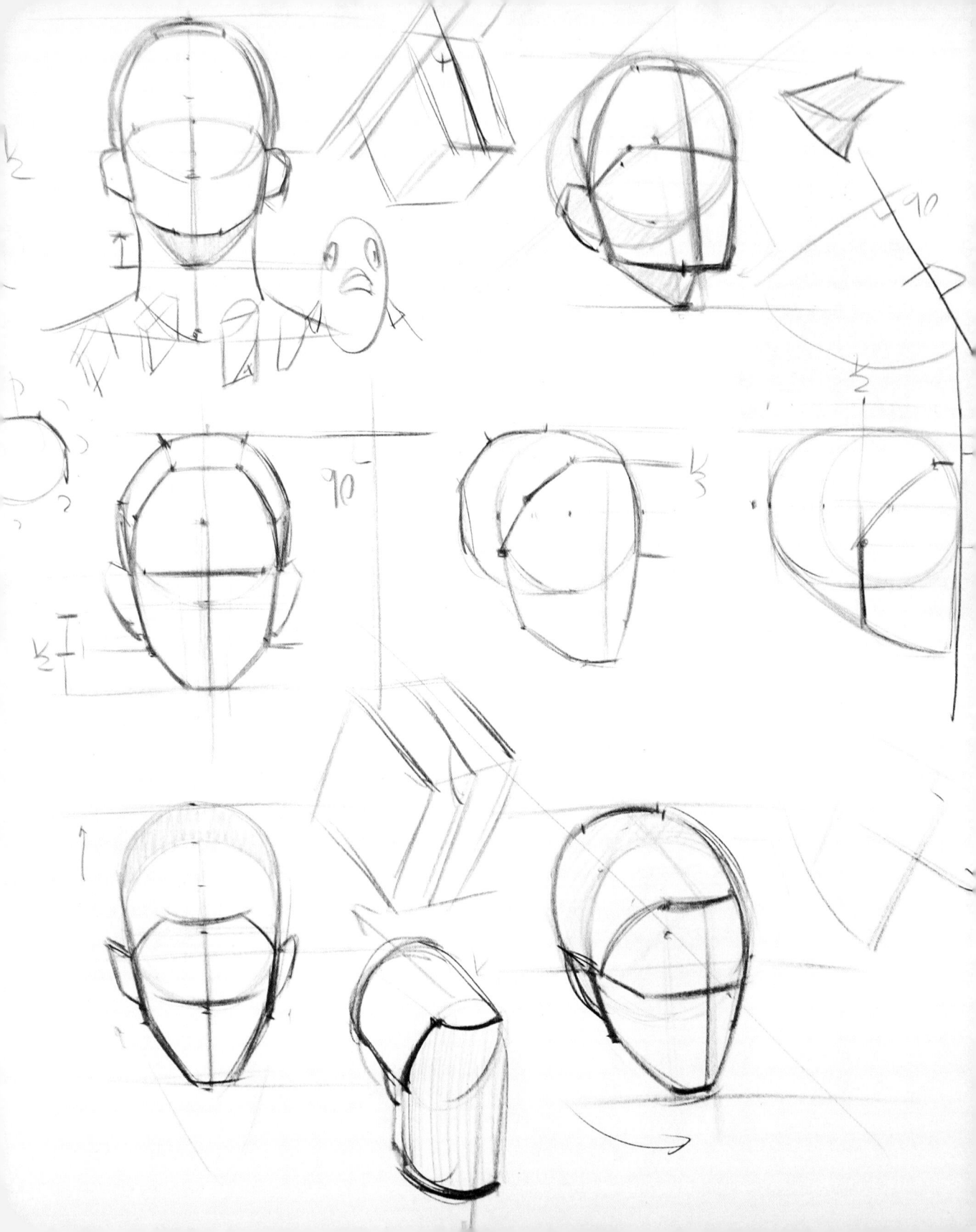

In the blank space above, practice re-creating Kevin Chen's template for the head, shown opposite.

OPPOSITE: Kevin Chen, *Head Rotation Demonstration*, 2017, graphite pencil on newsprint, 24 x 18 inches (61 x 45.7 cm), Analytical Figure Drawing course, Concept Design Academy

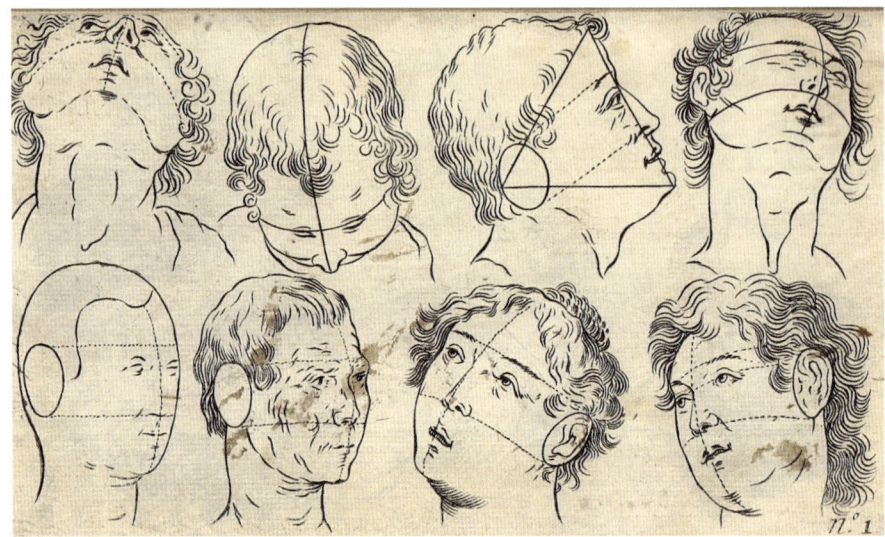

Placing the features

The skeletal structure of the figure is remarkably constant from person to person. These lines form a schema discovered and used long ago by artists who were interested in finding rules—universals—amidst all the changing forms in nature. Even though every person deviates in his or her own way from these ideal markers, the markers create a solid reference point.

Often, the first line is a centerline running from the widow's peak down between the eyes, through the bridge of the nose, and ending in the center of the chin. This line shows whether the head is tipping to the left, right, or is perfectly straight. To determine this, hold up a plumb line, pencil, or skewer to find the angle.

The second line runs horizontally right across the eyes, from the outer edge through the tear ducts. This usually marks the halfway point between the chin and the top of the head (if the head is facing you straight on).

Divide the face by drawing a line at the top of the forehead at the hairline, a second line through the brow, and a third line under the nose. These lines normally divide a face that is at eye level with our own into thirds.

Here are some useful rules of thumb for placing the rest of the features on an eye-level, front-facing portrait. Your model may or may not conform to these, but they give you a starting point from which you can check for comparisons:

ABOVE: Systems for understanding the structure of the head. The engraver is looking to identify thirds and how they change when the head tips. Notice the triangular block-in shape for the head in the top row, third from the left.

Engraving from *Polygraphic or the Arts of Drawing in Two Volumes,* by William Salmon, 1707

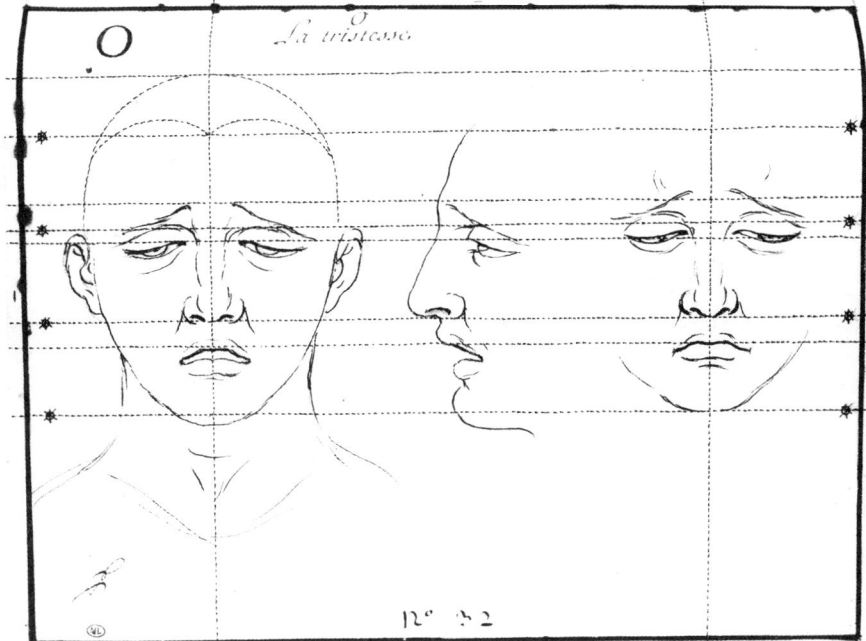

- The bottom of the mouth is halfway between the chin and the bottom of the nose.
- There is normally one eye length between both eyes.
- From the profile position, the center of the ear is halfway between the back of the head and the front of the face. The top and bottom of the ear align with the brow and bottom of the nose.

Consider Elizabeth Beard's drawing on page 110 for an example of how a portrait looks as a completed block-in. Notice how she located the proportional anchors by marking horizontal lines to the left of the face. By simply blocking in and finding the shadow shapes, Beard found the features without trying. You may also want to refer back to da Vinci's study on page 30 to see how checking angle alignments in the block-in stage helps you find the specific forms of the face.

To add the features themselves, find the shadow shapes and then render smaller forms. For example: to draw an eye, you may start with the shape of the brow ridge, the shape between the brow and the upper lid, and the cast shadow under the eye. Before you know it, you'll have an eye without effort. We draw the head just as we draw anything else: from large forms to small, general shapes to particular.

ABOVE: In this seventeenth-century drawing, the artist addresses rules of proportion that had been already noted almost two hundred years earlier in da Vinci's drawing on page 30. Finding the centerline and dividing the face into halves and thirds are standard departure points for portrait artists.

Charles Le Brun, *Features*, 1690, pen, black ink, and black chalk on white paper, size unknown. Image courtesy of Art Renewal Center

DRAW A PORTRAIT

Sketch this block-in of a head, using the progression discussed throughout this book. Note the horizontal dashes to the left of the head, which lock in the proportion of the features into thirds. On pages 112–113, start the portrait the exact same way and bring it to a finish.

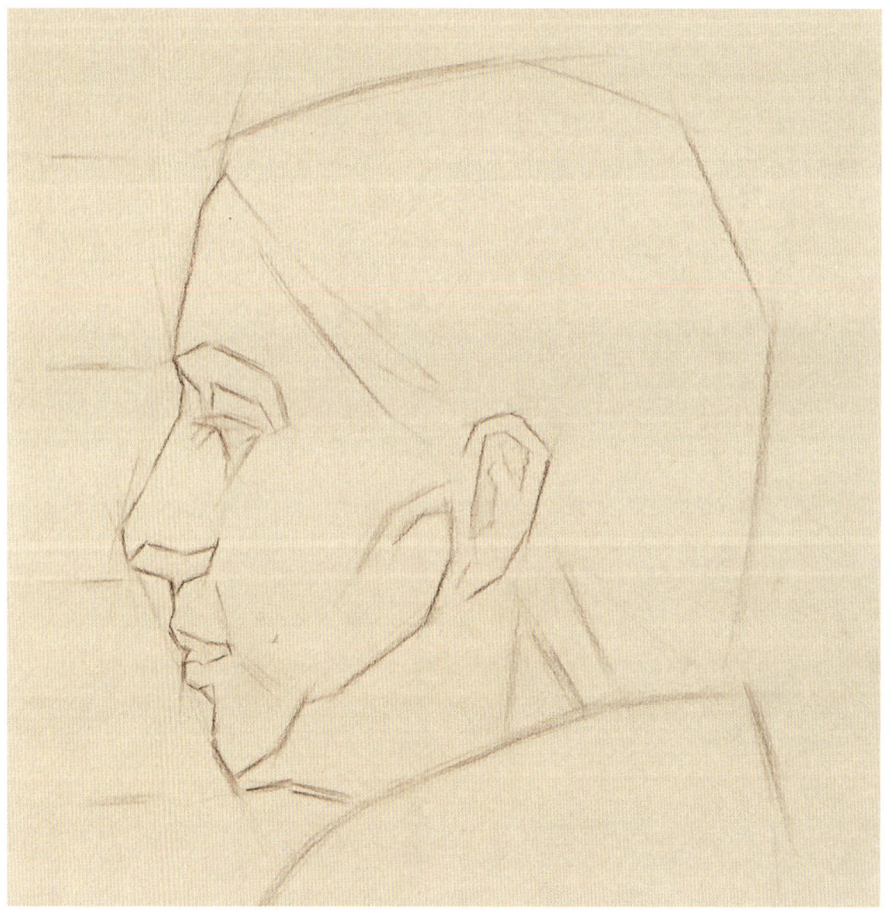

Elizabeth Beard, *Aubrey Stage One*, 2016, brown pencil on toned paper, 17 x 14 inches (43 x 35.5 cm)

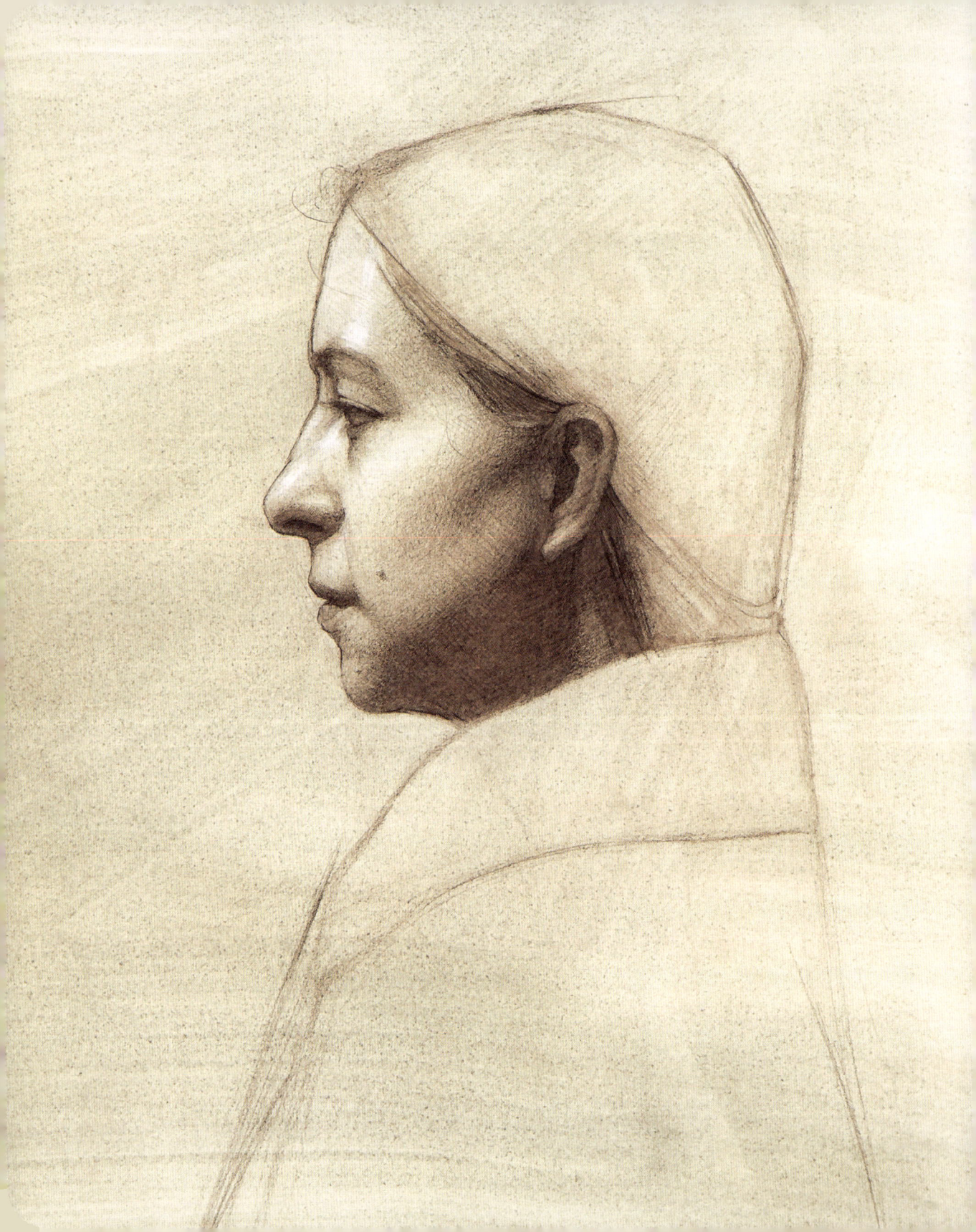

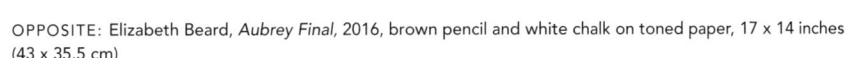

OPPOSITE: Elizabeth Beard, *Aubrey Final,* 2016, brown pencil and white chalk on toned paper, 17 x 14 inches (43 x 35.5 cm)

PRACTICE PORTRAITS

Sketch the following drawings here and on pages 116–119. Start by lightly sketching the block-in of the head, as you did on pages 110–111. Build upon that strong start to find the shadow shapes and render the form to finish the drawing.

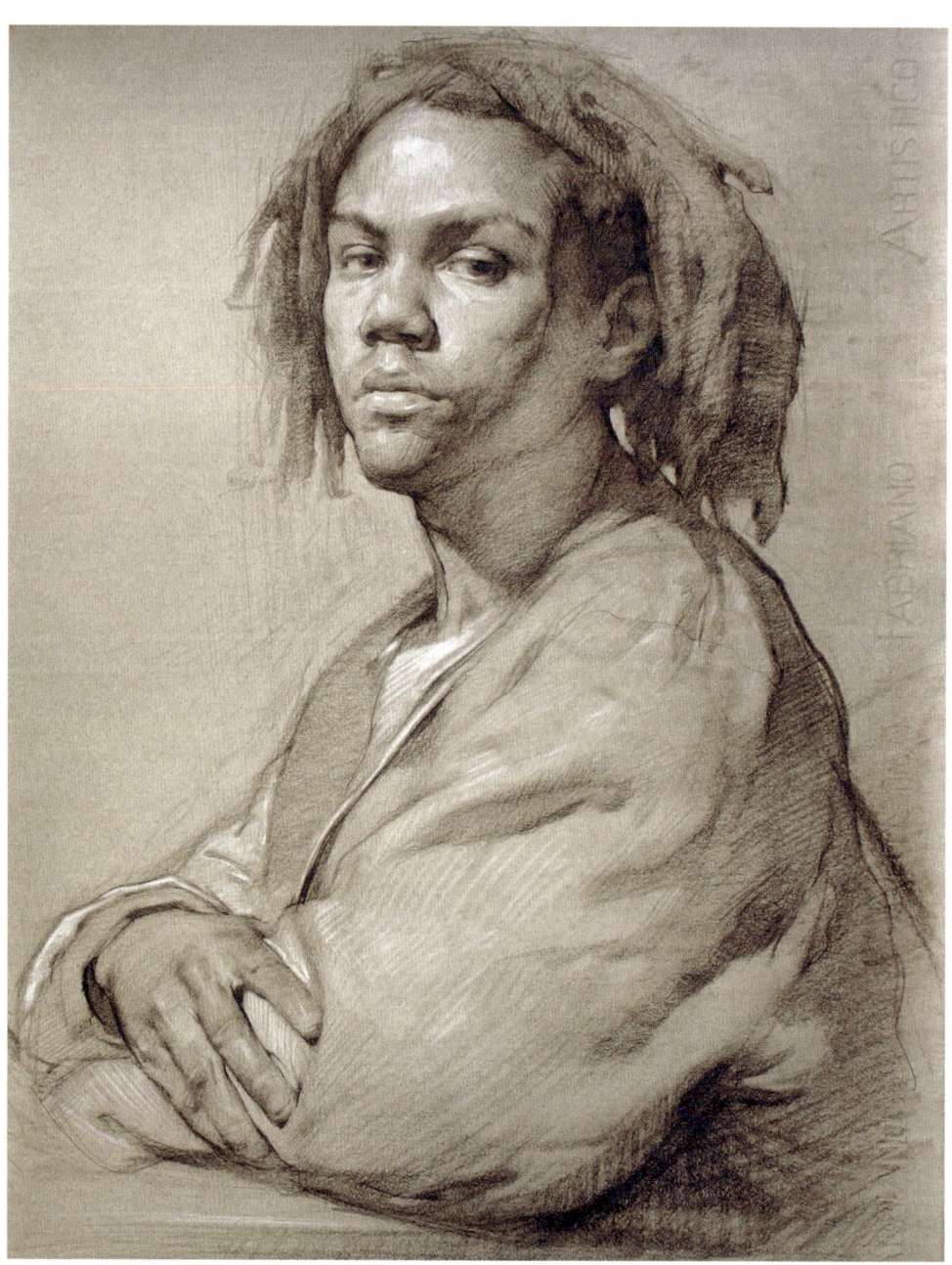

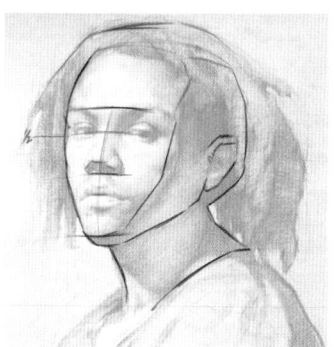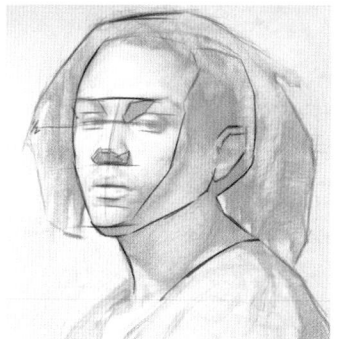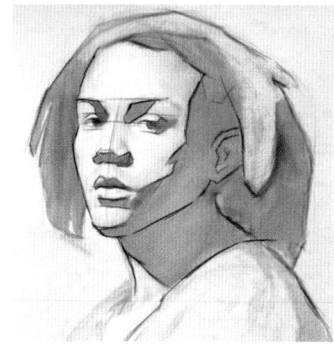

OPPOSITE: Colleen Barry, *Jamaal*, 2014, brown pencil on toned paper, 17 x 12 inches (43.2 x 30.5 cm), private collection

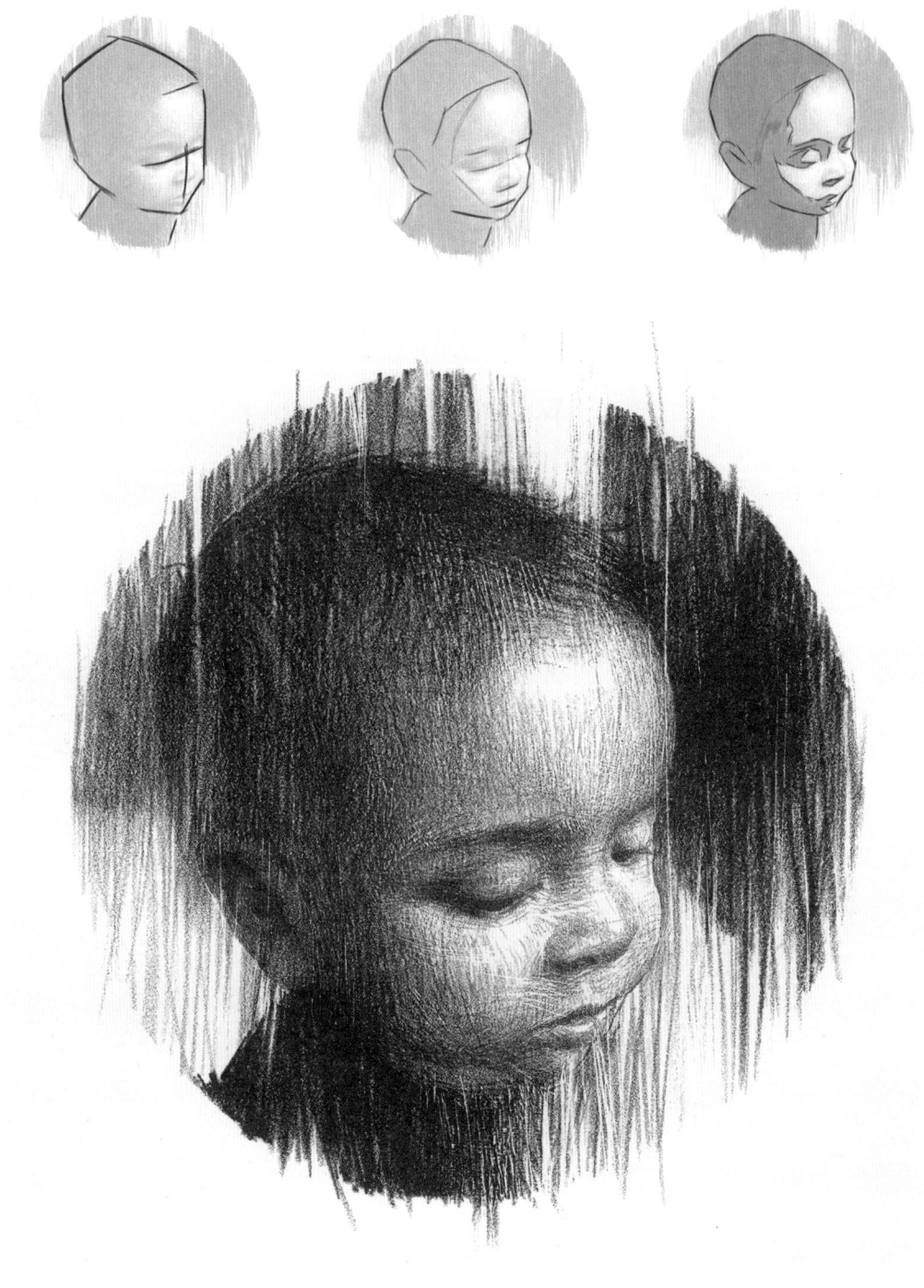

Irvin Rodriguez, *Los Infantes II*, 2016, ink on Hahnemühle Copperplate paper, 15 x 11 inches (38.1 x 27.9 cm)

OPPOSITE: Leonardo da Vinci, *Study of a Young Woman,* ca. 1490, silverpoint on prepared paper, 17 x 16 ⅘ inches (43 x 42.6 cm), Musée du Louvre. Image courtesy of Art Renewal Center

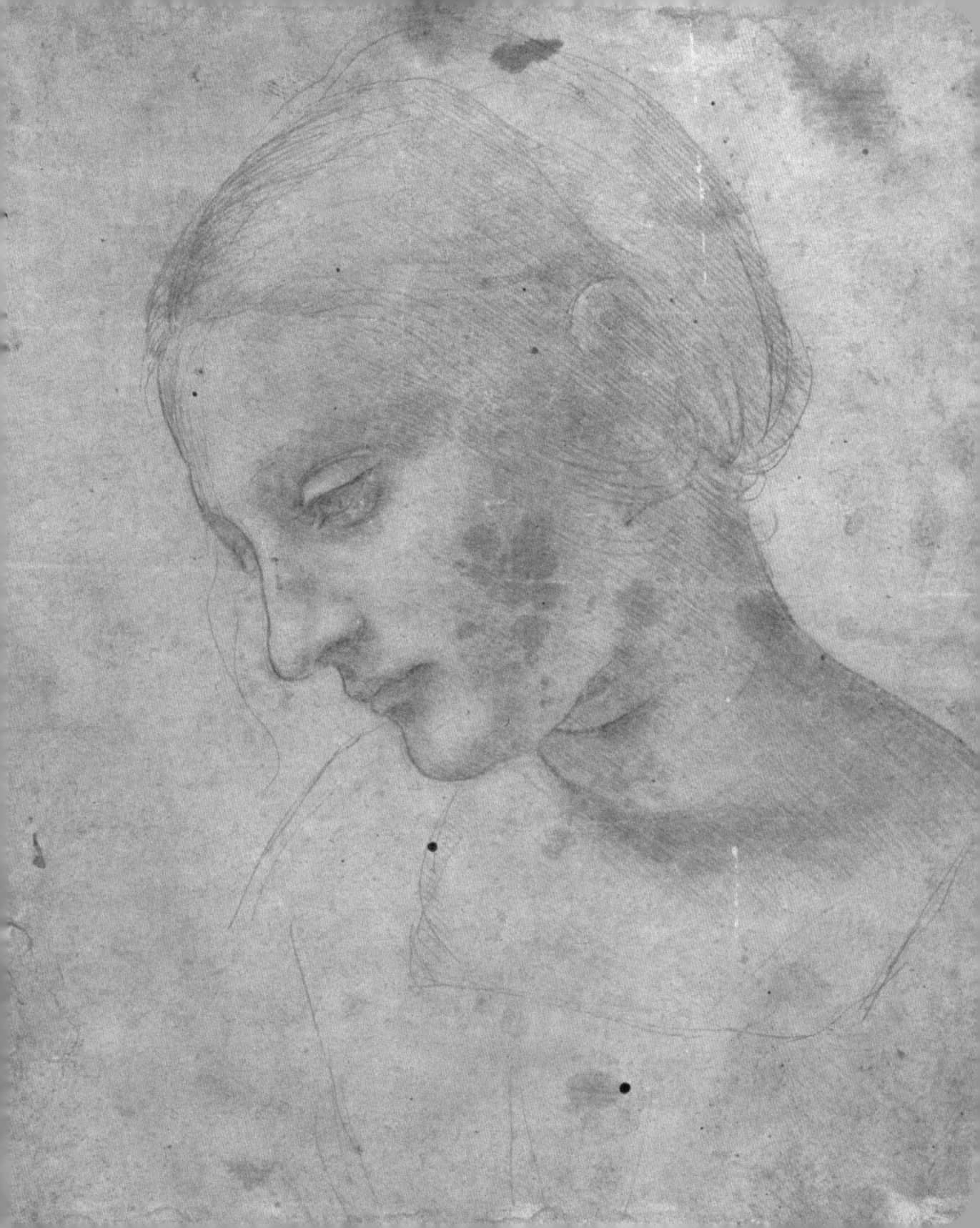

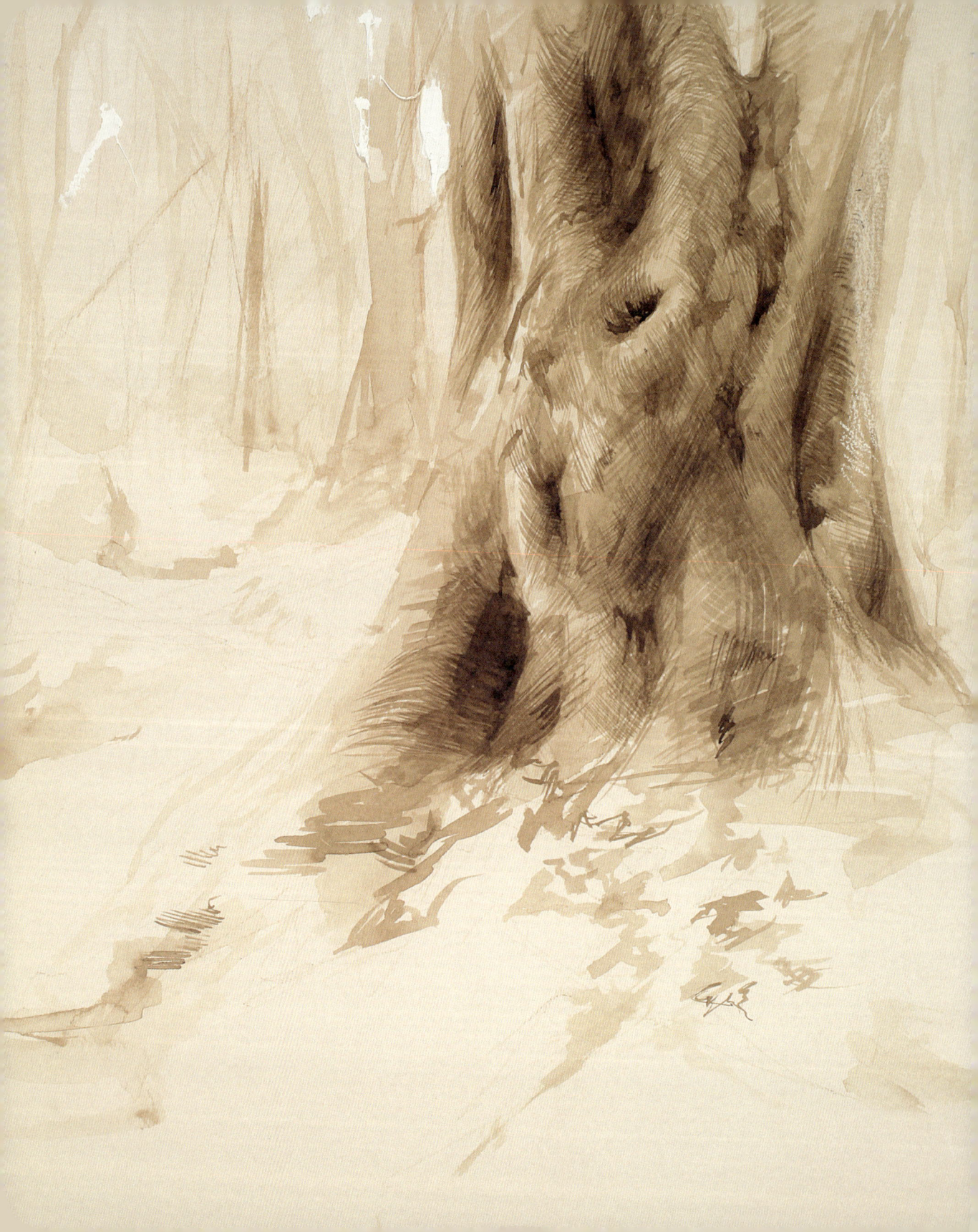

CLOSING

Never forget that every mind is shaped by the most ordinary experiences.
To say that something is ordinary is to say that it is of the kind that has made
the biggest contribution to the formation of your most basic ideas.
—PAUL VALÉRY

We are all familiar with museums that contain rare and beautiful things. These spaces and objects provide us with inspiration. Yet have you ever carefully inspected an object that has no value? Instead of a silver goblet at the Metropolitan Museum of Art, why not admire a dried leaf on your front steps, a bit of wild grass by the street, the reflection on a glass next to your bed, or a water droplet working its way down your screen door?

Sight is a powerful sense. I can see light from the Andromeda galaxy 2.5 million light years away without a lens, but sometimes I can't find car keys that are right in front of me. The best part of our life is but varying degrees of seeing. *How* we see is as important as *what* we see.

We can effortlessly identify objects the millisecond we look at them. Yet what happens if we keep looking at an object long after we have named it to ourselves? How about for five minutes, an hour, or ten hours? We start noticing. We see the object behind the name or the symbol as if for the first time. Deep looking, without idealization or habit, is grabbing hold of more life per square inch. This is the kind of sight that, in the hands of someone with skill, turns life into art—perhaps even into an object at a museum.

Careful observation is important for many art forms, not just drawing. Writers like George Orwell and Ernest Hemingway found that by observing their own lives as visitors rather than permanent residents, they saw things others missed. Orwell would sometimes silently narrate his life: "He pushed the door open and entered the room. A yellow beam of sunlight, filtering through the muslin curtains, slanted onto the table, where a matchbox, half open, lay beside the inkpot." Slow down enough to ask the question: What am I seeing? Rather than naming the object, describe the qualities and characteristics of what you are looking at. Now we move into deep seeing and the world of art.

OPPOSITE: Juliette Aristides, *Oak Tree*, 2012, walnut ink on paper, 12 x 9 inches (30.5 x 22.9 cm)

As we give sight our attention and time, the visible world becomes beautiful, meaningful, and memorable. To enter into a moment—to be bound up in the object of our attention and let the world fade around us—enhances our appreciation of life. How much do we value expensive things or experiences because we know they are rare, unusual, or costly? When something is important, we are told to "pay attention." How expensive is the petal of a flower that will never come again and is there only once, for our delight, in this space and time? This kind of seeing is not entertainment. There is no curator, no action, no plot, no director—just unmediated life and original experience. It is one of countless random arrangements in real life as it intersects with our own. The least interesting of our days is remarkable if we have the eyes to see it, if only, as nineteenth-century writer Thomas Carlyle famously put it, because each moment sits at the conflux of two eternities: the past and future. By learning to draw, we cultivate our sense of sight, and in the process, we begin to notice the mystery and deep beauty in the world that is ours.

BELOW: Juliette Aristides, *Oak Leaves*, 2012, walnut ink on paper, 9 x 12 inches (22.9 x 30.5 cm)

OPPOSITE: Julio Reyes, *Outland*, 2011, charcoal on paper, 28 x 20 inches (71.1 x 50.8 cm)

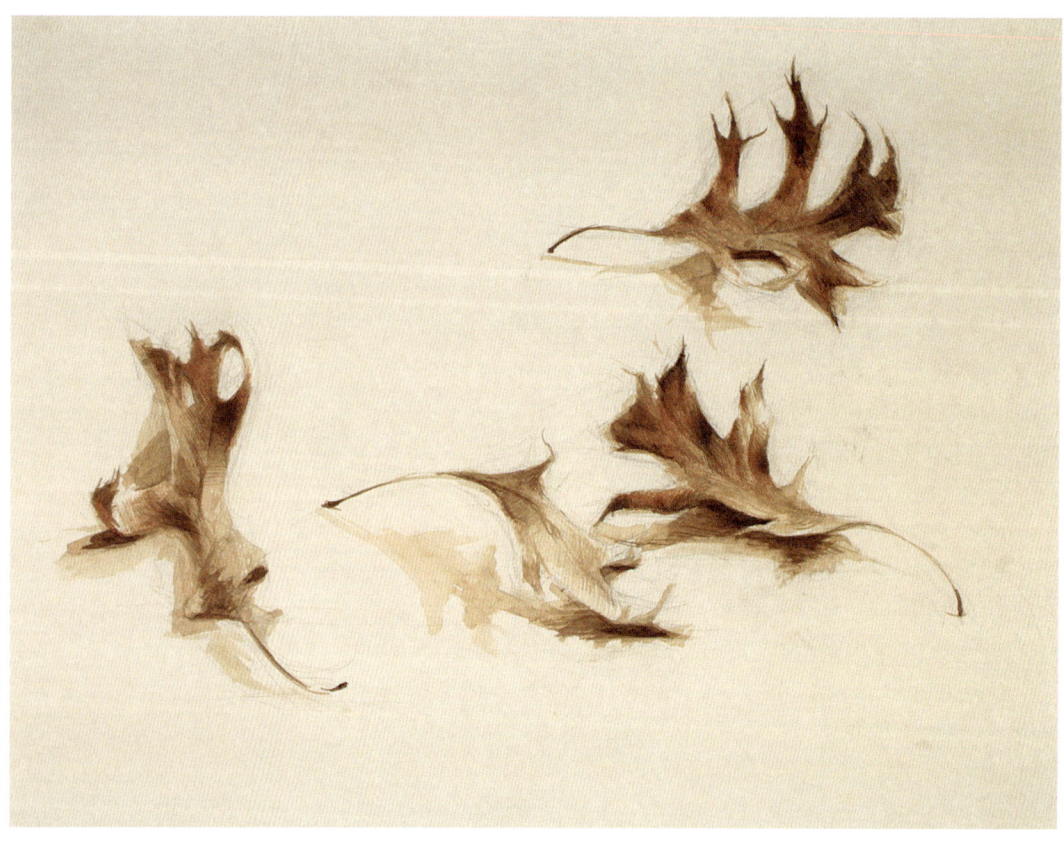

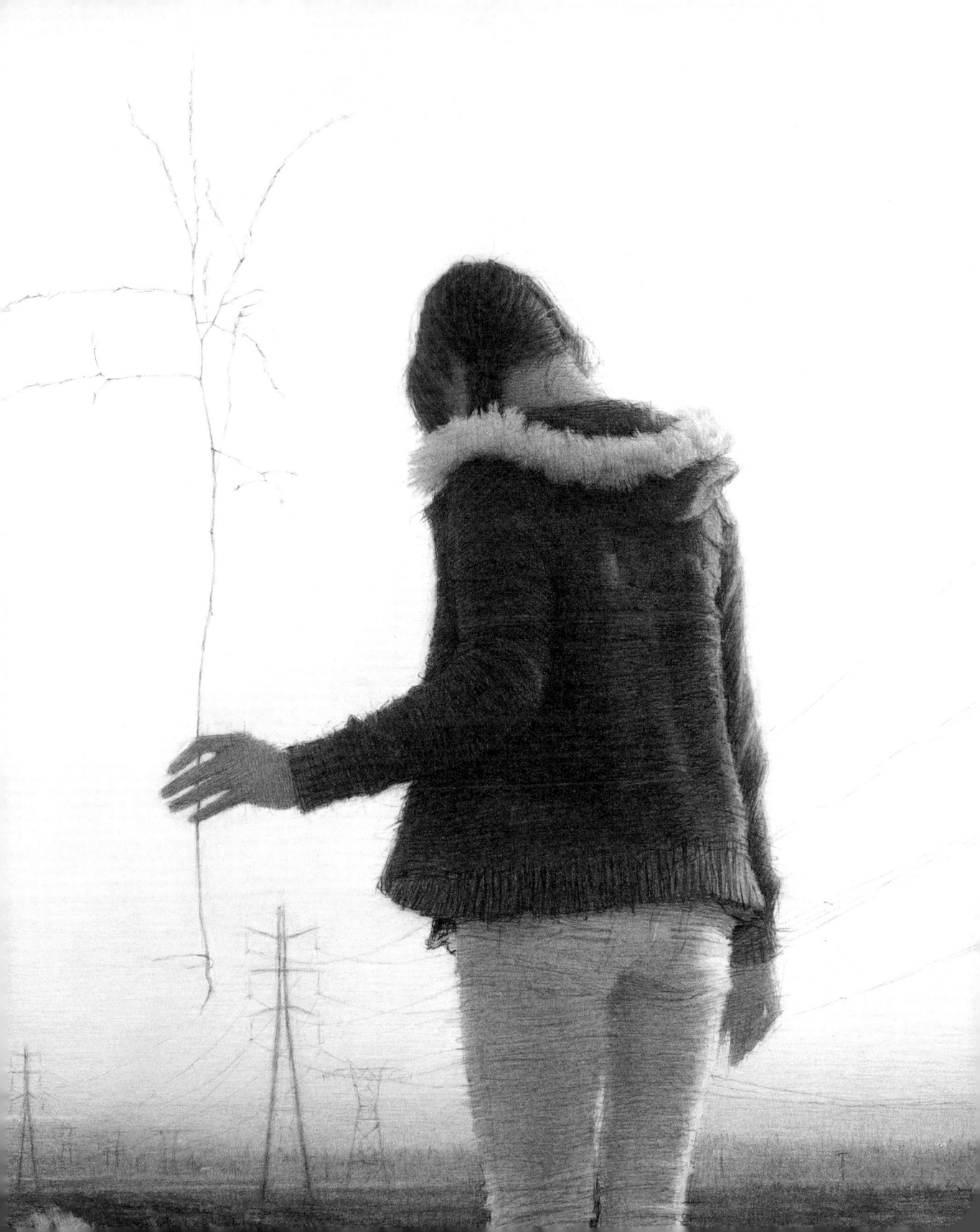

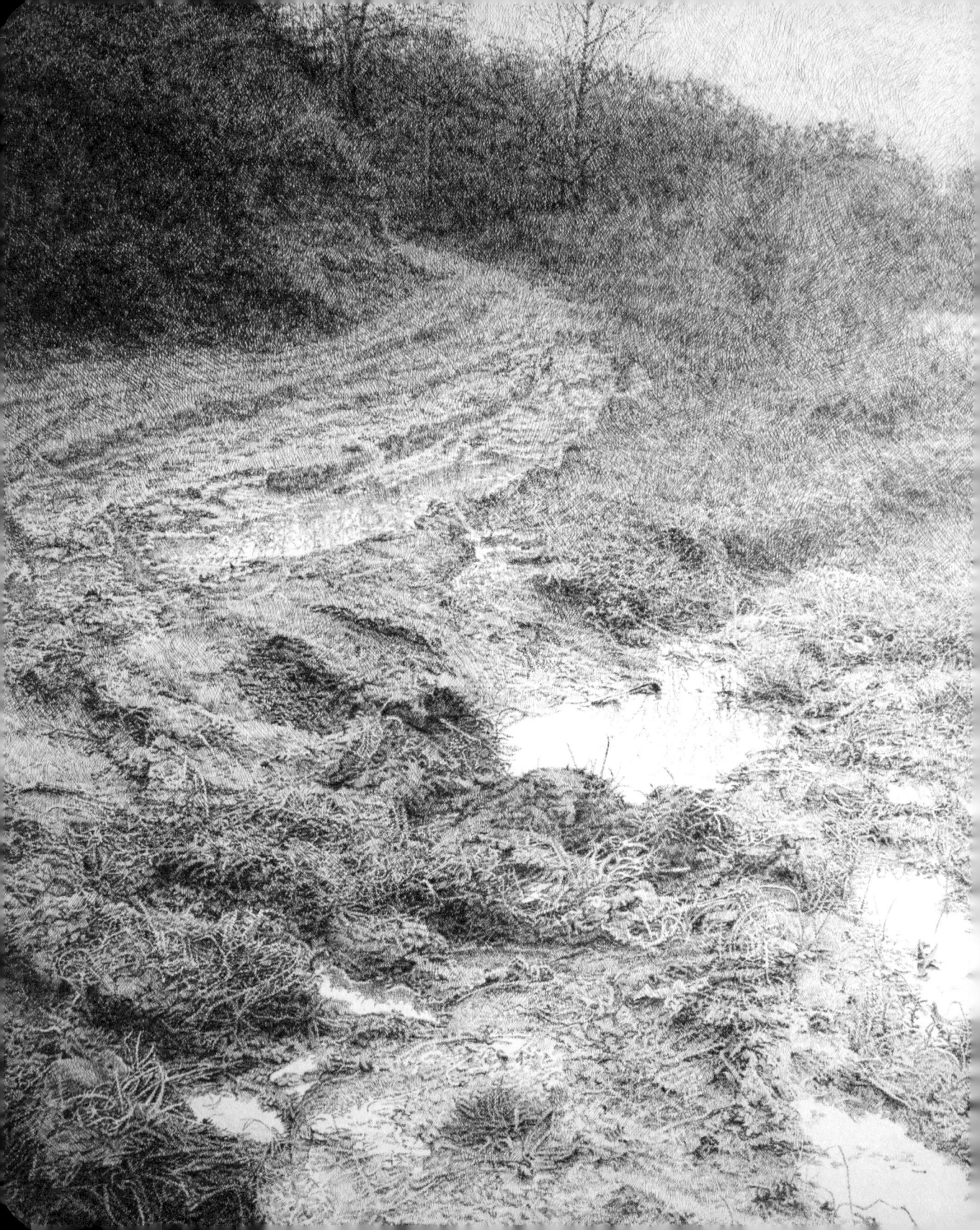

ACKNOWLEDGMENTS

My deepest thanks to those who worked to help bring this book to fruition. If you like this book, thank Will Berkowitz, who knew I should publish it before I did.

This book wouldn't exist without the faith of associate publisher Victoria Craven at the Monacelli Press. Thanks for believing in me and taking a risk to create something new. I am truly grateful to editor Julie Mazur Tribe for her clarity of vision and patience, and was lucky to work with Jennifer K. Beal Davis, a gifted designer who brought her elegant aesthetics to this sketchbook.

To John Zadrozny: once again, my friend, you made all things seem possible.

Ovidio Cartagena, your enthusiasm, creativity, and unstoppable work ethic made you the perfect partner to design the prototype and analysis overlays. You are gifted as both an artist and a designer.

Harriet Rubin and Paul Rosiak, thank you for being so generous with your time and proofreading the text.

To my beautiful sister-in-law Yael Levin, I am grateful for your hard work cataloging images.

This book could not have been made without the contributions from artists and students, whose drawings bring beauty and optimism into a world that needs it. Thank you to Ellen Sontra (lettersbyellen.com) for contributing her calligraphy. Thank you to the Metropolitan Museum of Art and the J. Paul Getty Museum for their open-source images. A big thank-you to the Art Renewal Center (www.artrenewal.org), especially founder and chairman Fred Ross and cochairman Kara Lysandra Ross, for art permissions and for changing the culture through its salons, scholarships, and the Da Vinci Initiative. Also, deep appreciation to fellow Da Vinci Initiative cofounder Amanda Theis for her tireless and passionate investment in the lives of teachers and students.

OPPOSITE: Yunfeng Zhu, *Muddy*, 2017, pen and ink on paper, 22 ¾ x 16 inches (58 x 41 cm)

INDEX

ABOUT THE AUTHOR

Juliette Aristides is an extraordinary draftsperson and artist with a deep and well-rounded education and solid commitment to the atelier movement. She studied at the National Academy of Design, the Pennsylvania Academy of the Fine Arts, and various private ateliers. She is now the director of the Aristides Atelier in Seattle, Washington, and is the co-founder of the Da Vinci Initiative, which works to bring skill-based art instruction into public education. Aristides exhibits in one-person and group shows nationally. Aristides is also the best-selling author of *Classical Drawing Atelier*, *Classical Painting Atelier*, *Lessons in Classical Drawing*, and *Lessons in Classical Painting*. She is based in Seattle. For more about the artist, visit her website at AristidesArts.com.

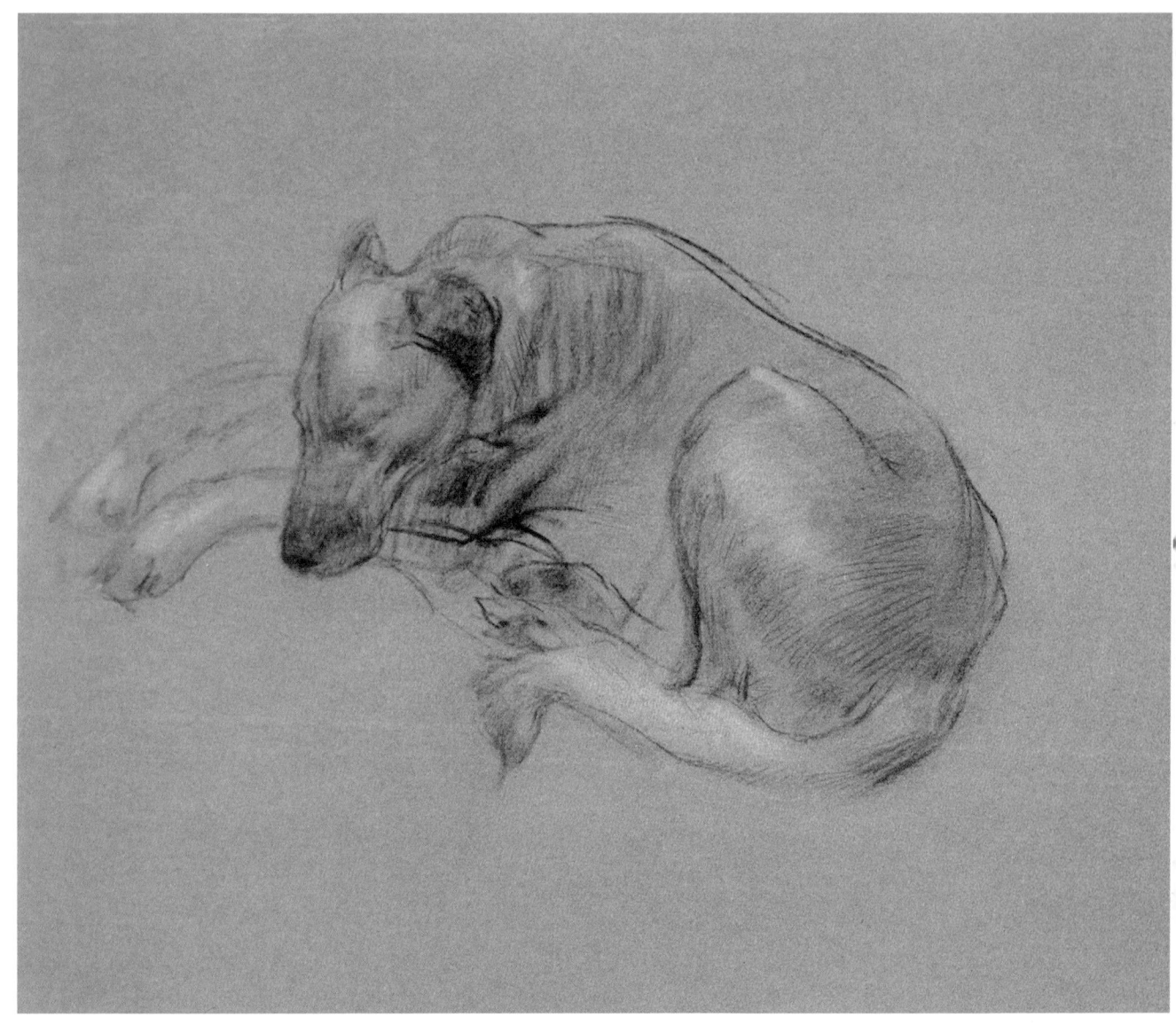

Sherrie A. McGraw, *Prince of Des Montes*, 2005, Conté crayon on paper, 13 ½ x 15 inches (34.3 x 38.1 cm)

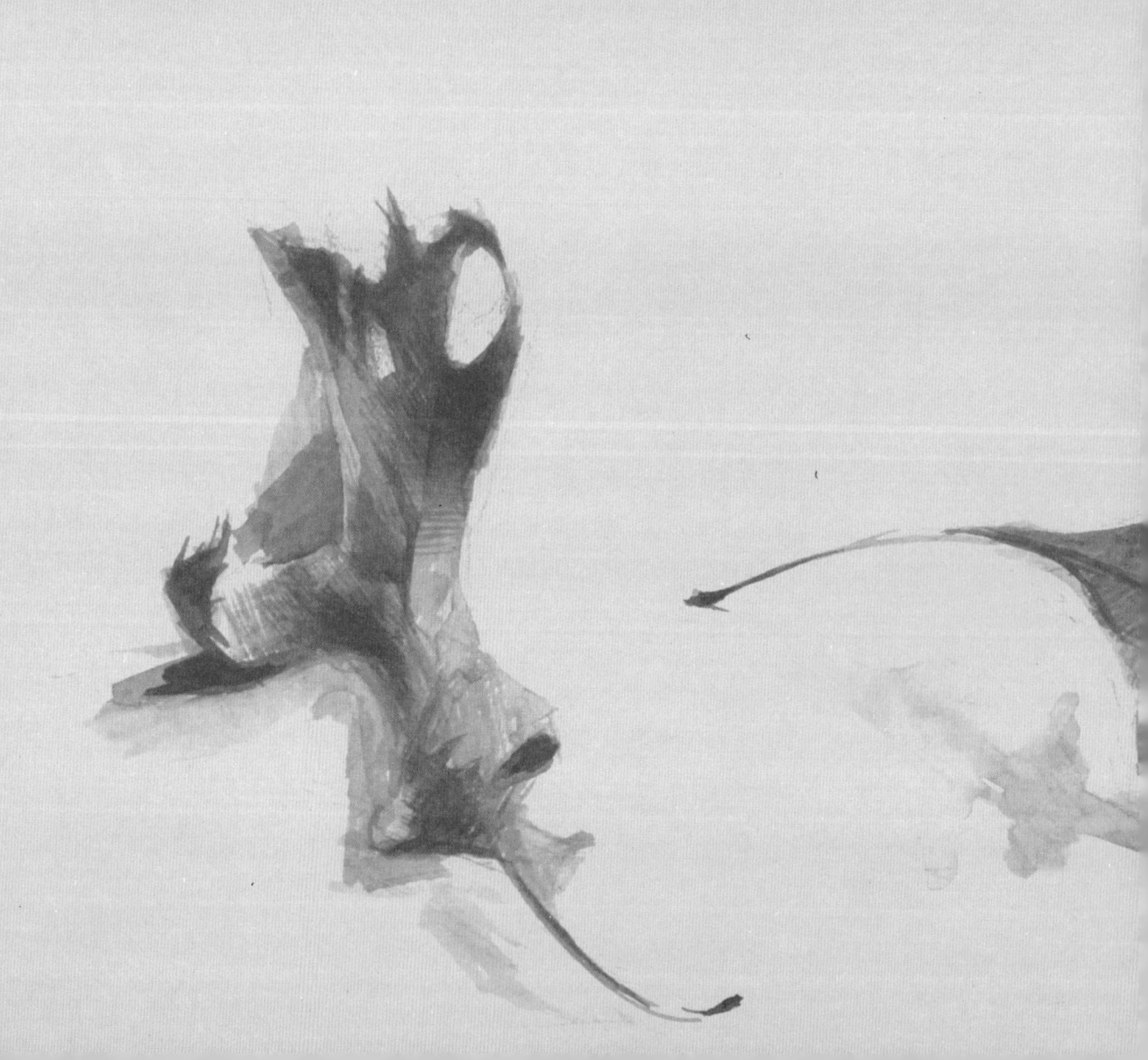